Scalpel To Sword

Scalpel To Sword

~⁀

Everyone Hurts Somewhere

Linda Lou Jones

Psalm 45:1: "… my tongue is the pen of a ready writer."

Unless otherwise indicated, all Scripture quotations are taken from the King James Version of the Bible.

Scalpel to Sword
Everyone Hurts Somewhere
ISBN-13: 9780980892925
ISBN-10: 0980892929

Website: www.LindaLouJones.com
Other Books By Linda Lou Jones: The Agonized Heart... No More. Available from Amazon.com and other retailers.
Available Soon: Final Request... Life Before The Cross; Praise The Lord... Life After The Cross; Rainbow Rider –Wanna Be Biker 40+ Takes Lessons; The Rent Is Paid –Journey From Scratch
Blog: https://www.rightlady.blogspot.com
Follow Me On Twitter: https://www.twitter.com/rightlady7

The evening prior to my appointment with the surgeon, I said,

"Lord, what *about* all of this?"
He said, **"It won't be easy,
but I will stand beside you
every step of the way,
and I will see you
through."**

He did exactly that.
With much gratitude, I dedicate this book
to my best friend, Savior, and Lord:
Jesus Christ.

Thanks,
Linda Lou
**Psalms 23:4: "Yea though I walk through
the valley of the shadow of death
I will fear no evil; for thou art with me;
thy rod and thy staff, they comfort me."**

Preface

〜

G'day, World,

WHEN I GOT serious with God, He knew it, and He got serious with me. The first scripture He quickened to me was **Psalm 45:1: "... my tongue is the pen of a ready writer."**

When you are sixteen hundred miles from home with no family, and the doctor finds a large, cancerous tumor, you find out what else is on the inside of you, too. Pressure brings it forth. Inspired poems bubbled up from within, birthing my perspective as well as that of my best friend, Jesus. **Nurses read the poems, wept, and asked for more.** Walk with me through the valley of the shadow of death.

Do you know someone who has cancer? Do you know people who have things they wish they did not have to deal with? They need this book. When my eyes and ears were opened in a new way, perspective took on a whole new dimension. As a passionate overcomer, I got my breakthrough and learned the root cause of the cancer.

You will have the opportunity to emerge from the valley changed. Time is ticking. I tell it all in these frontline accounts. Cancer survivors have been there, paid their dues, and—in my case—been promoted out of there. Let's take a walk together through the valley. Key word: *through!*

Family and friends become victims when someone is diagnosed with cancer because it touches their lives, too. I have one son, one daughter, one granddaughter, and three grandsons, all of whom are "almost" perfect! I'm French Canadian, born in Quebec, living in Ontario, Canada, and the United States. What you are about to read is more than poetry or testimony; it contains meat for the soul, answers to questions, and keys to unlocked areas. I am excited to share with you each page.

If you know someone who died from cancer, and you do not understand why he or she did *not* get healed, listen up. Since I lost my father, a cousin, a next-door neighbor, a hunting friend, and one chemo-patient buddy to cancer, some questions needed to be answered. It took years, patience, and earnest digging, but answers were received.

When you read the answers, you will be challenged. There always is an answer. It is just not necessarily what one may think or expect, but there is an answer, thankfully. *Perspective* is a key word also, so whatever you are hurting about, there is something you can do. Find out what it is.

I pray that as you read, you will have ears to hear the voice of the Lord as clearly as I did when I asked, "What *about* all of this?" Also, I pray that you will obey His voice because, as stated previously, time is ticking. If you happen to be deaf, you are not excluded from hearing God's voice because God speaks to your heart, so be listening. God bless you as you read this labor of love, *Scalpel to Sword*. This cancer survivor just happens to be using her life experiences as a platform from which to write

First, though, a heartfelt, sincere thank-you to the following people: **Ms. Donna Bentley and family** for the love, prayers, open heart, and open home; also, to my *Apostolic Father* through whom I continue to become perfected *with truth*, and for each intercessor who prayed for me. Once again, my heartfelt thanks and appreciation!

Contents

1

Me...or...God *in* Me

~~

I don't want to be old.
I don't want to be laid up.
I don't want to be a burden to anyone,
And I certainly do not...
Want to die!
I do not like the depression
That has come at me recently.
I am trying to sort things out,
Be realistic, be wise, be brave.

Since I had over half of one lung removed
And was diagnosed with cancer,
Life has changed so much.
Or is it life—is it existing?
I think that is my choice.
It is not a tough decision.
I choose life.

No matter what, I choose to press on courageously.
God's plan is unfolding day by day,
Hour by hour, minute by minute.

So, although I have major changes going on
In my health and I am planning to move sixteen
hundred miles
From Texas, United States, to Ontario, Canada,
I find myself having to lift my chin up
Purposefully, now and again.
I long to spend time
With family and friends.
I am glad to be moving in the spring.
It seems when I look to the future,
I can go just so far; then it seems I hit a wall.
When my heart wants to dream on,
I seem to draw a blank.
This grieves my spirit.

I'm a woman who wants to believe in God for restoration.
I'm not going to lie down and die.
Yet I need confirmation from Him
Whether there is still time for me on this earth
To receive the restoration promised me.
I do know God can do more in one year
Than I could do in ten years.
Nevertheless, I'm asking for confirmation.
To be really, really, really honest,
I'm not so sure I'm ready for dating
Let alone marriage...
So if God has someone for me,
He'd really have to rank high
To get as much as a second look from me.
Meanwhile, I'm trying to keep my chin up
And asking God for much grace.

I write straight from my heart
Because being honest is easy for me.
The walls are down.
I feel really, really small
On the inside of this aging tent
But my spirit man acts ten years younger
Than I really am.
Sooooooooooooooooo
I am going to just be me
And if someone likes me, good.
If not, fine.
I'll still be me
Because I like me,
And Jesus does, too.
And if I'm good enough for Jesus,
Then for sure I'm good enough for anyone.
I chose Jesus, and if He's got someone,
He can choose and work it all out.
I trust Him.

These are the thoughts
Rolling around in my head
And in my heart.
I haven't written much lately
And believe it is time—
Time to be yet more vulnerable
As I do what I said:
"Be me."

No wonder I feel so small.
Maybe subconsciously I'm thinking

The smaller I am, the less conspicuous I am;
Therefore, the fewer the potshots.
When one has been wounded as much as I,
There comes a reaction—
A defense mechanism,
If you will—
In an effort to protect oneself.
The flesh dies hard.
I find myself withdrawing from the front lines,
Content to not be so conspicuous.
I'm still God's servant.
He is giving me wisdom and understanding.
Somehow, deep in my spirit,
I just know
It is going to be okay.

God has bathed me in peace.
I know Jesus will never leave me.
My hand is in His all the time.
As we walk on the water together,
There is a purpose for each step we take.
The burdens are on His shoulders, not mine.

Together we press on with hope and love,
At times even dancing on the water joyfully.
Being in His presence is really all that matters.
Circumstances cease to be mountainous,
As in the arms of my Lord and Savior,
Love surrounds me completely,
And such unconditional love

Never fails.
Only Jesus can give such contentment,
As well as joy, peace, and grace
In the midst of my feeling
Like I'm in the eye of the tornado.
Jesus is the answer.
He knows me better
Than I know myself.
"He works all things together for good,"
According to Romans 8:28.

It is Christ in me:
That is my hope of glory.
It is no longer I who live,
But Christ
Who lives in me.
I'll be me
And ask God to use me
In whatever way He chooses.
My goal is to be used
To bring glory to God;
That's why I'm on this earth.
"With God, all things are possible."
It is no secret what God can do.
Little is much when God is in it,
And God…is in…me!
Glory to God!

This was written 3.28.03, twenty-three days after I had lung surgery.

P.S. Bottom line: Joshua 1:9: "Have I not commanded thee? Be strong and of a good courage; be not be afraid, neither be thou dismayed: for the Lord thy God is with thee whithersoever thou goest."

2

Nothing

~⌇

I write right.
Why?
Because I write from my heart—
A heart in which Jesus dwells.
No wonder I'm not at a loss for words.
Living with Jesus
Means living with life itself.
There is no death or defeat in Him.
He does not visit occasionally.
He is not a guest.

He dwells eternally with me.
We are one.
Divinely done.
I am the vessel, the pen.
Jesus is the ink
That flows through.
Nothing is too hard for Him to do.
Nothing.

3.28.03
Jeremiah 32:27: "Behold, I am the Lord, the God of all flesh: is there anything too hard for Me?"

3

Valley Experience

~~

The doctor specializes in radiation treatments.
When I left his office,
I knew in my spirit, deep within,
I had a decision to make:
Would I receive twenty-five to twenty-eight treatments
In a five- to six-week period,
Or would I decline and trust God completely?
It takes faith to trust the Lord.
I can't please God without faith.
Since the doctor's odds are a fifty-fifty chance
Of being 10 percent better,
Yet at the same time, he says I may not have any cancer,
I don't have to make a decision.
God made it for me.
I sat in my pickup truck in the parking lot
Pondering over all of this.
Simultaneously I saw flashbacks:
Faces of several women who were in the waiting room.
One had no hair and wore a cute cap,
But when our eyes met and I smiled warmly,
She lowered her eyes in shame.
It was obvious from her dress—so cute—

She did all she could to compensate for the loss;
Yet inside, she did not…have victory.
I still have peace in my heart.
I opened my Bible and read
Job 22:28: "Thou shalt also decree a thing
And it shall be established unto thee,
And the light shall shine
Upon thy ways."
I felt uplifted and hopeful upon reading this verse.
Again, I realize it requires faith.
That is something I do have.
Tomorrow I have a 10:00 a.m. appointment
With the chemotherapy doctor, the oncologist,
If the office referral is processed.
So, I prayed, "God, if I'm not to get chemo,
Please stop the referral from going through."
I rebuke fear, doubt, and unbelief.
Peace within is my umpire.
Guess what? At 4:30 p.m. today,
I called the doctor's office.
They did not have the referral.
Praise the Lord.

3.31.03
FYI: There were changes; read on.

4

Getting in the Flow

The wind blew in circles,
Lifted my hair to and fro
As I sat in a lawn chair
In the backyard.
I found a quiet, secluded spot.
With my coffee mug handy,
And my Bible too,
I thought it would be
A good thing to do—
Taking time to read the Word
And enjoy the sun and grace too.
But on the other side of the fence,
Someone had other thoughts of what to do.

"I heard a loud bark,"
From a huge dog
Just as I was about to park myself.
Then the wind got stronger and distracting.

I moved to the front of the house.
Surely, I was not asking too much.
The neighbor's American flags waved repeatedly.

The spring buds on the trees pushed forward proudly.
The children's windmill turned and turned.
The flowers were just beginning to emerge
From the damp soil because it had finally rained recently—
And Amarillo, Texas, isn't noted for having a lot of rain.
The solid blue sky is changed suddenly
As a jet plane leaves a white path in the sky.
It is now 10:00 a.m. on Tuesday, April 1, 2003.
I can't help but wonder
How many homes invite the presence of the Lord
Let alone how many souls are saved.
The atmosphere in each home differs so much.
Everyone has his or her own individual standard raised.
Some raise it for Jesus, who is Lord of their lives.
Some raise it for sports, which they put number one.
Some are workaholics, driven daily
Rather than led by the Holy Spirit
And able to keep a healthy balance.
Some homes have the TV as their focal point;
With others, it is the dinner table
Where they commune, and gather.
Laughter rings forth often,
And hearts are drawn to return often.
Others seldom eat together
Let alone enjoy a home-cooked meal.

They're working hard, hurrying and scurrying about,
Leaving mealtime as a hit-and-run episode—
No doubt because no one likes to dine alone.
Some folks are hospitable,
Using their homes to bless others often.

With others, that is something seldom done.
They likely have not questioned their hearts as to why,
Yet if the truth were known,
They think everything has to be shipshape
Before they can entertain.
Then there are those who compare
What they have with others.
If they feel they don't match up,
Pride causes them to withdraw and back off.
Jealousy and pride are thieves, enemies.

The home I live in is so special.
A single parent, her two daughters, and one granddaughter
Invited me to live with them.
We hardly knew each other, other than as acquaintances.
I moved out of my apartment, put things in storage,
moved in.

Since that time, I was ill on and off for weeks.
Recently I was diagnosed with lung cancer.
I'm in my fifties, divorced, no family in Texas.
And forget trying to figure out my age:
Age is just a number.
Suffice to say I am old enough.
☺
I had major surgery; over half of one lung was removed.
Now I am recuperating,
No chemotherapy or radiation needed.
This family have never once complained
About the sacrifice it has been for them
To have me here.

They have never condemned me about anything.
In fact, their hearts are so big
They gave me the master bedroom and bath!

They treated me as one would treat Jesus.
It is so important as Christians
To do whatever we do as unto the Lord.
I have observed them do so daily
For three and a half months now, without fail.
I am not on welfare,
Not on food stamps; I don't have life insurance,
Or CDs—no savings account either.
I gave away my furniture.
I am 100 percent dependent on God.
He called me into full-time ministry in November '02.
A lot has happened since then.
God proved Himself faithful.
He arranged that I would have medical coverage
Just three weeks before an x-ray
Revealed a large tumor.
He used people to help me.
I did not ask anyone for money.

I was given money to pay for vehicle insurance and gas,
As well as storage-building fees—and even to get my
nails done.
God does give us the desires of our hearts
When we delight ourselves in Him.
Some "religious people" may say

That's a frivolous expense, a waste.
I don't let them be my judges.
Rather, I smile and know God knows how
To improve my self-esteem.
When I feel good about myself—
And I do—and when I look good,
I do well and am productive.
Rather than being critical,
I have a heart full of praise and thankfulness.
Why?
Because I recognize the hand of God.
He talks to me daily.

We dine together daily.
We pray together daily.
We do everything together.
Jesus is my best friend.
Jesus is my spiritual husband.
The Holy Spirit has taught me
That when the world comes in…
He leaves.
I work at being sensitive to His presence
So as not to grieve Him in any way.
I do not ever want to hurt the Lord.
He has done so much for me.
When I can sit anywhere
With paper and pen and write and write and write
As the words flow like a stream
From within my heart,

I am so happy and content—
As I am right now.
Why? Because I am using the talent
God gave me as a writer.
I am allowing the Holy Spirit to inspire me
To write word after word after word.
It's almost like I set my head aside
And simply listen to my heart.

As I step out in faith and write one word,
More words come.
It's kind of like turning on a water faucet.
I'm the vessel; the Lord is the ink flowing through.
So I pray the words I've written
Will result in you searching your heart
As to what your priorities are and
What kind of standard you've raised in your home.
Is there a welcome mat?
Is there laughter? Is there love?
Is there fear? Is there condemnation?
Is there manipulation? Is there control?
Abuse is not God's way of life.
As you reach out to Jesus and draw nigh,
You'll find He's been there all the time,
Waiting patiently for you to acknowledge His presence.

He wants to lift you up and help you,
Give you answers to your questions,
Give you hope for the future,
Unfold His plan for your life,
Heal you, deliver you,

Put you back together again.
And not only that...
He wants to make something beautiful
Out of your life.

He'll teach you how to build your home
On a solid foundation.
He'll help you lower the walls
And risk being vulnerable again.
He'll heal the hurts and make you stronger
In those areas than ever before.
He'll do that and so much more,
So slow down and be still in His presence.
He has things to say to you.

He'll speak to your heart,
Perhaps even audibly,
Through His Word, the Bible,
As well as Christian TV, radio, books,
Friends, and family.
There's no limit to what He can do.
Cast your care upon Him.
If the burden you're carrying is too heavy,
It is because Jesus paid the price
To carry it and set you free.
Was Calvary in vain?
I pray not.
Each day that passes,
The clock is ticking down.
Do not procrastinate.
You don't know how long you have.

Neither do I, so let's occupy till He comes.
Don't look back; look up. Jesus is coming soon.
Rejoice in His wonderful presence.
Abandon yourself to Him.
All else will follow: Matthew 6:33.
He will never let you down.
Jesus lives.
And only *Jesus saves*!

4.1.03

Matthew 6:33: "But seek ye first the kingdom of God, and His righteousness; and all these things shall be added unto you."

5

A Resurrected Voice

Someone said, "Did you quit singing?"
My heart sank with conviction.
It was true; my song was gone.
I came home and prayed and repented—
Asked God to restore because I really,
Really do like to sing Christian songs
That uplift Jesus Christ.
I got my microphone and songs out,
Took as big a breath as I could
Since having lung surgery,
And started to sing.
In my heart, I was glad I knew
It did not have to be perfect.
Just sing it to the Lord
Because it sounds beautiful to Him.
I tried, and I cried, and I tried some more.
The more I practice,
The stronger my lungs get.
It is good exercise for me
Because I have to learn how to breathe again.
I can do all things through Christ who strengthens me.
That's what the Bible says.

God is restoring, and I give Him glory.
My voice has been resurrected!
(At least partially.)

4.1.03
Philippians 3:10: "That I may know him and the power of his resurrection, and the fellowship of his sufferings, being made conformable unto his death;"

6

Just Do It

~~~

Knowing I am to give things away
Is what helps me to keep pressing on
Even when my chest hurts,
I'm feeling short of breath, or
My body tells me it is tired.
My head hears the battleground in my mind.
I park my loaded pickup in the driveway,
Come in the house, and lie down.
That is when I don't want to think
About anything at all.
I just want to close my eyes
And sleep…that's all.
Then I remember the rest of the boxes
Waiting to be removed from the storage building.
The garage is pretty full

Even though I am reorganizing daily.
It seems endless; I counted seventy boxes.
There are about thirty boxes left to bring.
I do not have the strength to do it
Let alone the desire.

Plus, it is up to eighty degrees Fahrenheit now.
Yet it must be done.
So, I go to the answer,
God's Word, and speak the truth:
"I can do all things through Christ
Who strengthens me."
"Whatsoever He says to you, do it."
"Obedience is better than sacrifice."
"Rejoice in the Lord always."
"In everything give thanks."
"God blesses those who are kind to the poor."
"In everything give thanks."

"He helps them out of their troubles."
"The joy of the Lord is my strength."
"The Lord is thinking about me right now!"
I try not to allow a lot of questions,
Such as wondering where everyone is at
When I could use some help.
Instead I focus on the Lord
And follow through with giving things away.
I have continued to separate chaff from wheat
And sow seed after seed by giving.
It started after the separation began—
Plus, I've been tithing and giving offerings
For twenty-four years.
God is bringing in my harvest.
I obeyed His instructions.
The best is yet to come.

4.2.03
FYI: The family I lived with moved from an apartment into a house when I had surgery. This meant I could move my boxes out of my large storage building and into their garage. I had already given away the furniture and was now continuing to downsize and reorganize just one month after lung surgery, so it was done gradually.

7

Called

~

After enjoying a hot shower,
Hot coffee, and toast,
I sought the Lord for direction...
His plan for me for this day.
Each time I headed for the door,
My peace came back to me.
I kept seeing our troops in Iraq
And knew what the Lord was trying to say.
He wants me to bloom where I'm planted.
Pray, pray, and pray some more.
That's why I'm Spirit-filled.
That's what my heavenly language is for.
I pray for the perfect will of God
For people at war thousands of miles away.
Realizing the battle in the natural
Is also a spiritual battle, I pray.
I'm a soldier in God's army,
Called to pray and pray through.
As I intercede, God intervenes.
It's really not hard to do.
I could sit in the hot Texas sun
On this beautiful April day

Or go for a walk to get exercise
While simultaneously I pray.
Yet as I obey the leading of the Holy Spirit,
I find myself focused on praying
For those at war in Iraq, and that's it.
No distractions—just praying with my King.
Jesus is the King of Kings and Lord of Lords.
He is praying, too.
It is an honor
To be an intercessor.
It is something we are all…called to do.

4.3.03
1 Thessalonians 5:17: "Pray without ceasing."

8

Restrictions and Cooperation

~

God forgive me,
But I'm starting to feel
Like a prisoner.
I can't do the physical work
To get things out of the storage building.
I can't go buy a plane ticket and leave.
God has called me back to Canada to live,
Yet I'm in Texas, sixteen hundred miles away.
What am I to do?

I'm in pain, fighting loneliness and depression—
Not to mention the frustration
Of not being able to do what I want:
The publishing God has called me to do.
I try to keep my eyes on Jesus.
I try to encourage myself in the Lord.
He's collected all my tears and preserved them.

He has recorded each in His book.
He is for me; I am trusting Him.
He will see me through the valley.
I have faith in my future.

Somehow God makes a way where there is none.
I remind myself of the truth:
That He can do more in a day
Than I can in a year.
I need my family, God.
I want my daughter and son and brother.
I need their support.

I don't want to waste precious hours and days
Living like this.
God, please help me. I can't do anything on my own.
I ask for favor from You.
I'm burning bridges behind me as You requested.
Help me, Jesus…I need someone to lift my hands.
I'm just being honest, real.
Grace always comes when truth is told.
Give me grace and help me to be brave.

Help me not to look back.
I turn my faith loose.
The past failures are in the past.
My intimacy with You has increased.
I've obeyed You and am climbing up spiritually.
I've sowed to my future.
You have anointed me.
My hands are open to receive
Because I've let go of all.
My faith went through death, burial, and resurrection.

It is all right to cry about what I don't have yet.
In fact, it is good to be able to cry.

Since lung surgery, I couldn't until now.
It means I can't take a deep breath yet
And feels like trying to drink from a straw
That has a hole in it.
But even a little cry relieves pressure.
It doesn't change the circumstances,
But it does make a difference.

I will shine again—
Shine for Jesus through and through,
Shine and be clamorously foolish.
God is restoring my body
As I rest in Him.
I am recuperating nicely.

God is strengthening me.
Praise the Lord.
This too shall pass!

4.3.03
Psalm 42:5: "Why art thou cast down, O my soul? And why art thou disquieted in me? I hope thou in God, for I shall yet praise him for the help of his countenance."

9

Compromise versus Commitment

~)

When people call themselves Christians
Yet live like the heathens,
It grieves the Spirit of God
As well as the spirits of the Christians
Who do have clean hands and pure hearts.
How do I know?
Because I have done both.
I learned to trust God and
Stop doing things my way.
His ways satisfy completely.
A right relationship with God
Will see anyone through any trial.
So why do some people rebel,
Turn from God, and reach into darkness?
Why do they lose their fear of God?
Why is quicksand so appealing to them,
Especially when they've taken that route before?
With sin comes deception.
That is the fruit of sin.
Plus, the wages of sin are death.

Why would anyone choose death
When Jesus paid the price to give abundant life?
How it must hurt God the Father
When His children turn their backs on Him.
Yet because God loves everyone so much,
He gives everyone free will.
He will not violate that free will.
If someone chooses to live in the pigpen,
He will allow it.
For a time He will lovingly woo that person
Back into His wonderful presence,
But only for a time—not forever.
There comes a time when He won't strive with man.
I wonder if that is why He called the intercessors
To stand in the gap for the backsliders,
To stand in the gap for the deceived, sin-ridden souls.
Who better to intercede
Than those who have been in their shoes?
The truth is written in one of my songs:
Simply stated, I've never seen
A happy backslider.
There's no such person
On this whole earth.
The devil's thrills are temporary.
He's got nothing good that lasts.
He knows he's going to hell,
And he wants to take you there, too.
But...I've got good news:
Jesus hasn't given up on you!
His love is drawing you closer,
And His love always breaks through!

Because Jesus loves the backslider,
And He knows who you are.
He wants to lift you up, so…
Don't run far!
When you learn how much He loves you,
You'll fall in love all over again.
Jesus doesn't change, you know.
His love is falling on you like rain.
He's been faithful.
Will you be faithful too?
Because Jesus really does have
A perfect plan for you.

He'll give you lots of love and peace.
He'll fill you with His joy.

You'll have a brand-new life with Jesus Christ.
You'll be busy in His employ
Because there are a lot of backsliders
On their way to hell.
Go forth in His name.
You'll do very well…
If you walk, talk, and dine with Jesus
And walk in the shoes of the intercessor.
Or
Do you walk in the shoes of the backslider?
Let the Holy Spirit search your heart
Before you decide…
Because if there is deception,
You did not know it before…
So, let God show you what He sees.

His viewpoint is much broader.
Nothing is hidden from Him.
Let His love penetrate
To the depths of your spirit
As He floods you through and through.
He still saves, heals, and delivers.
He did it for me.
He'll do it for you.
He is no respecter of persons.
Will you yield 100 percent to the Holy Spirit?
Let Him do what He needs to do?
It is breakthrough time once again.
He does not want you restricted in any way.
Get ready; you're breaking through.
Nothing is too hard for God to do—
Absolutely nothing!

4.5.03
John 8:36: "If the son therefore shall make you free, ye shall be free indeed."

10

Occupy till He Comes

~~~

It's so wonderful the way God reveals things.
As I am writing poems,
I see the faces of people who are praying.
It touches my heart immensely,
Especially because some of those people live
Sixteen hundred miles away.
Surely the Spirit of the Lord is moving
All over the world, and there is no distance in prayer.
If we really believed our prayers were getting through,
A lot more praying we would do.
I'm talking to myself and to you.
Let's press in and pray through.
We know Jesus is coming again soon.
I sure do not want to be found
Watching TV when He comes—
Not when there is so much work to do.
Souls are dying daily.

I do not want their blood on my hands.
I pray you feel the same way.
So let's keep our feet shod
With the preparation of the gospel of peace,

Keep our armor on as we go forth,
Shining for Jesus—bright lights.
We have much to look forward to
When Jesus is Lord of our lives.
He brings restoration in every area.
He is by our side always,
Leading us, loving us, protecting us,
Enjoying our times of walking together,
Dining together, communing together,
Praying together, dancing together,
Laughing joyfully together, and just being ourselves
As we drink in His agape love—
Vessels that are full of the Holy Spirit
And are continually being refilled
Because we take time to pour out to others
Who are in need.

We drink of the living water
That we may minister to others
From the overflow, as into the world we go.
Mind you, if you choose to deny Jesus,
That is your decision.
You can go to hell…if you want to,
But He made a way for you to go to heaven,
And Jesus is the only way.
So, I pray you choose Jesus and you obey
Because only *Jesus* saves!

4.5.03
Matthew 5:16: "Let your light so shine before men, that they may see your good works and glorify your Father which is in heaven."

FYI: It was difficult to find a comfortable position after surgery due to not yet being able to lie flat, on my tummy, or on one side. I was on pain pills for five months.

11

Truth Hurts

If someone is disrespectful to women
When he or she is single,
It will not change
When he or she is married.
When someone does not submit to authority,
It won't change when he or she becomes wed.
When someone single approves of sexual sin,
It will also happen in the marital bed.

Morals do not change overnight.
Everyone knows deep within
What is wrong and what is right.
Most just choose to relabel sin.
They call it "being in a relationship,"
Yet it is fornication or adultery.
Let's call a spade a spade and not play games.

God hates every kind of sin, and so should we.
If we love God, we should hate sin;
Otherwise we'd be compromising.
When we stay focused on Jesus,
Good fruit we bring.

He is somewhat like a magnet,
Drawing us closer all the time—day and night.
We quickly resist temptation to sin
Because we instantly want to do what is right.

The more we take a stand for righteousness' sake,
The easier it is to stand tall,
Knowing within that Jesus is the reason we don't
compromise.
We're so glad when we answer His call.

Jesus is calling you.
He's calling you closer to God's heart.
He knows what you are going through.
Will you trust Him to give you a new start?

He never condemns anyone.
His love goes much deeper for sure
'Cause He sees the hurt in your heart,
And Jesus is the sure cure.
He's forgiven many backsliders already,
Washed their sins away with His blood.
If you knew how much Jesus loves you,
You'd inundate Him like a flood.

Facing reality takes some maturity.
Do you manipulate and control?
Do you say one thing and do another?
Do you ever set a goal?
Are you concerned about only you?
Do you blow your cool

And reveal what is really inside you?
Do you act like a fool?
Does anger occupy a lot of your life?
Do you do anything about it?
Or do you think it is simply okay
To go about throwing a fit?
Do you try to change?
Do you want to?
Do you care enough to try?
What are you going to do?

You already know
You can't do it alone.
Jesus is waiting for you to reach out to Him

Rather than a phone.
Friends don't know you deep inside.
Few even care.
Love is near; try Jesus.
He'll be with you everywhere.
You don't even like yourself anymore.
You infect others negatively.
Your mouth is like a sewer.
Your body is trapped in sexual sin—you are history!
It is your life going down the drain
Because of decisions you make daily.
To become kind, loving, respectful, complete,
A right relation with Jesus there must be.

It is time to grow up.
Make an about turn, 180 degrees.

Make Jesus Lord of your life.
Choose to make Jesus the one you please.
You will never regret serving Jesus.
His ways really satisfy.
Chin up—it's your time for victory.
No need to cry.

Life and death are serious business.
I pray you choose life every day.
Jesus is the author and gives abundantly.
Be brave, be bold; Jesus is the only way!

John 14:6: "Jesus saith unto him, I am the way, the truth, and the life: no man cometh unto the Father, but by me."

12

More Ways than One

Everyone has a track record, including me.
Perhaps that is why I'm hesitant
To receive some thoughts that keep coming,
Which I know did not originate from me.
I do not want to be deceived or misled.
I've been seeking God as to His plan for my life.
Thoughts came to me of a particular gentleman.
He is praying for a wife.
Yet when it comes to the future,
I'm not so sure I want marriage.
In fact, I recall saying years ago,
"I'll never marry a farmer or a preacher."
God's humor is better than mine.

Part of me questions whether I am good wife material,
Yet is that for me to say?
No wonder these thoughts
Caused me to pray and pray and pray.
I want God's perfect plan for my life.
I am praying for restoration in every area of my life.
In doing so, I've realized that includes marriage.
Better be careful how I pray. (Whew.)

What can I say?
No wonder I even hesitated
To put this in writing,
But since the thoughts were gentle,
And I was nudged several times,
I knew I had better commune with the Lord
Because I believe He is communing with me.

I have asked Him to reveal more of His plan.
Seek, knock, ask…help me, Jesus,
In more ways than one!

4.5.03
Luke 11:9: "And I say unto you, Ask, and it shall be given you; seek, and ye shall find; knock, and it shall be opened unto you.

13

Spring Changes

~⌿

The Texas sun is warm and welcoming.
Though it is April 5, I am getting a sunburn.
Leaves are on the trees already,
Gently blowing in the breeze.
Birds are chirping time and again.
Colorful blossoms appear on other trees.
Spring has arrived once again.
Signs of new life are everywhere.
Life comes from God.
He is the giver of life,
Whether it is to humans, fish, animals, or birds.
He is the author of life.
Seasons come and seasons go.
I see changes in the trees, grass, and flowers.
What matters more is that there be
Changes in me.
As I am made in the image of God,
I want to be changing daily.
My desire is to be more like Jesus.
He is changing my address soon.
That means I am changing, too, .
As roots are lifted in preparation.

Moving from one country to another
Is not easy to do,
Especially when it is sixteen hundred miles away.

Not only do I need to relearn street names
After being away thirteen years,
There are also major changes in climate,
Not to mention changing from Fahrenheit to Celsius,
Gallons to liters, spelling words differently in Canada
Than in the United States—
Plus a lot of changes in expressions,
Accent, and attire—cultural differences, basically.
Though it is a spiritual battle,
And I am determined to stay on fire,
I realize many changes are coming,
And I want to be prepared as best as I can.
So, I pray and pray and pray some more.
Realizing people look different thirteen years later,
I pray I am diplomatic,
That I do not put my foot in my mouth,
That I think before I speak,
That I stay full of the Holy Ghost,
And that God can and will use me
For His glory.
I want to be a blessing to others.
That is why God taught me
The importance of being transparent.
I have no secrets from God.
My heart is totally open, and He resides within me
Not as a visitor but dwells with me for eternity.
It is easy to be transparent

When you have nothing to fear—
When you do not lie, so you need not cover up sin.
It is easy to be a Christian
When Jesus is Lord of your life.
His love and peace and joy permeate your very being.
You become very sensitive to the Holy Spirit,
Knowing that when the world comes in, He leaves.
Sharp discernment is given for a reason.
God supplies every need.
Though the battle is severe, I will still trust God.
He is a God who cannot fail!

4.5.03
Isaiah 52:12: "For ye shall not go out with haste, nor go by flight: For the Lord will go before you; And the God of Israel will be your reward."

14

Pleasing Jesus

~⁓

My mind wants to read the Word of God.
My hand keeps pushing the pen to write more.
Once I am in the flow of the Spirit of God,
It is like there is no door—
Just a wide, flowing river,
Brimming with life and flowing freely,
Beckoning me to swim farther,
To write more and more
As I trust the Holy Spirit, my Teacher,
Who is my Guide who lives within.

It matters not that I am swimming upstream.
It matters not what others do.
What matters is that I step out in faith
And continue doing what God called me to do.
He's called me to live by faith.
I know the voice of my Shepherd.
He said to me one word: **"Come."**
When I looked up at the sandy beach,
His face I did not see,
Because He was standing on the water
Beckoning me... **"Come."**

If Jesus calls you to walk on water, you can.
He does not ask you to do anything
He has not first prepared you to do.
He is a God of order.
In fact, He is a perfectionist.
He is absolutely without flaw.
He is my example to follow.
He is my Mentor, my all in all.

I pray I don't waver or fall.
I pray I please Him as I answer His call.

4.7.03
John 12:26: "If any man serve me, let him follow me; and where I am, there shall also my servant be: if any man serve me, him will my Father honour."

15

Four to Six Months

The words keep echoing in my head—
Words spoken by the chemo doctor to me.
He said, that is how long I need chemo,
Not to mention radiation therapy.
Yet with the same mouth
He told me there's
A fifty-fifty chance of my being 10 percent better.
Also, two of the four lymph nodes
Are cancerous,
Which means there is cancer.
I cannot cry.
I seem to be numb.
I am not angry—
Disappointed, perhaps.
Yet I must look at it spiritually.
Jesus paid the price
For me to be healed.
His Word says, "I was healed."
Deep within, as I face truth,
There is a grieving and tiredness,
Yet I feel like I need to arise
With righteous indignation,

Take a big breath, stand tall,
And fight the good fight of faith—
Resist the devil and all illness and disease,
Speak the promises of God, and
Stand on His Word.
I must—
Because I do not want to die.
It is not my time.
Yet why haven't I done so?
I need to cry.

There is something else
I am aware of that concerns me.
I have not been able to settle down,
Get into God's Word, press in,
Even read, let alone study.
I know that is not good.
It is like a withdrawing...
From God.
Now that really makes me want to cry
Because I do not ever want to do that.

So why can't I study?
Am I upset with God subconsciously?
In my spirit, I know illness does not come from Him,
So once again I say,
"Help me Jesus, help me a bunch.
I need a breakthrough.
I must get the victory in my spirit.
Then I will see it manifest
In the natural."

It feels like I am a soldier,
Fighting this battle all alone.
I have people praying for me,
For which I am thankful.
Yet when it comes to a support group,
No one is there; few phone me.
I am alone a lot,
Facing Goliath and trying to be brave.
But God knows people need people.
I have to talk to someone
Who can help me.
Father, thank You for divine
Appointments—timing, too.
I can do nothing without You.

You made it clear to me:
I am not to take chemo or radiation.
Hearing from You helps me so much.
I do have such incredible peace in my spirit,

Yet this floodgate must open
To allow the tears out.
It is true that You did not let me down.
I am very aware You have honored Your Word
Because if I had not been confessing it,
Quite likely the doctor would have removed
All of my lung, not just half.
The Word says, "According to your faith
Be it unto you."
That is reality, too.
So, help me get from this day

To the next,
Not existing but living for Jesus.
I feel like I cannot move forward
Until I get help spiritually.

I must reach out,
Not wait for people
To come to me.
Lead me, guide me, protect me.
Give me wisdom and understanding.
Give me what it takes
So I can press on
And do what You have called me to do.
Give me a perfect heart
Filled with love and peace and joy.
I choose life—Psalms 91—long life.
I praise you, Father God,
For my breakthrough
In Jesus's Name.

4.9.03

Psalms 91:14–16: "Because he hath set his love upon me, therefore will I deliver him: I will set him on high, because he hath known my name. He shall call upon me, and I will answer him: I will be with him in trouble; I will deliver him, and honor him. With long life will I satisfy him, and shew him my salvation."

16

New Memories

~~

Tonight was a special evening.
Two couples I have known
For several years now
Met at the restaurant,
And we all dined and fellowshipped together.
It was just great.
Then we went to one home,
Had coffee, and fellowshipped some more.
They took pictures, too.
That was when I wondered
If they thought it would be
The last time they saw me.
In my spirit I wouldn't blame them
For wondering...
Yet I prayed I would see them all again
When they visited in Ontario someday.
I was given a leather briefcase
To carry my manuscripts
On the plane.

That really blessed me!
God supplies every need.
Thank You, Father,
For new happy memories.
You really do
Know how to please.

4.9.03
FYI: I had doctor's orders not to fly until six weeks after the
lung surgery.

17

Roller Coaster

~

I looked at the title
Of the last poem: "New Memories."
I thought of what is happening today
It felt like a roller coaster.
When I awoke my throat was so sore,
I was coughing, and my chest hurt.
Not good—so I drove to the clinic.
When I got in the office,
I started to cry, telling the nurse
About lung surgery and cancer.
I appreciated her hug and compassion.
Only God knows what goes on
On the inside of someone
When fear and illness attacks.

I blow my nose, chin up,
And wait again for my name to be called.
I expect they will give me medicine:
Antibiotics or whatever.
I am wondering about the PET scan
Scheduled for Tuesday.
I need to have it done.

Then my son can book my flight to Canada.
Interesting how one thing dovetails another.
Somehow, in the midst of it all,
I just know God is here with me.
Oh, how wonderful to lean on Him,
To draw peace and love and comfort.
True—I cannot see Him,
But I sure know He is here.
I feel His sweet presence.
Fear is gone.
All may not be well in the natural,
Yet the Word says it is, so I'll believe God.
I opened my Bible at random after writing this,
And these are the two verses that jumped out at me.
They were very comforting indeed.
Praise the Lord.

John 10:14: "I am the good shepherd, and know my sheep, and am known of mine."

John 11:4: "When Jesus heard that, he said, This sickness is not unto death, but for the glory of God, that the Son of God may be glorified thereby." ☺

18

What a World

What is this world coming to?
I had an open bottle of prescription medicine—
Painkillers to use after lung surgery—
In my purse when I went to the clinic.
I set my purse down next to me
On a shelf as I used the pay phone.
Then I remembered a courtesy phone,
So I left the pay phone and used it.
Later, as I waited for my new prescription
To be phoned in,
I realized my partial bottle of pills
Was gone from my purse.
Gone—just gone.
I backtracked,
Checked with the clerk as well
Then called security.
That is when I was told
They were having a big problem
With drugs disappearing.
I suggested they post a notice
On the countertop
At the receptionist's desk.

I came here at 9:30 a.m.
Now I cannot leave until I get the refill.
The doctor's office reopens at 3:15 p.m.
Long day or what?
Praise God I have my wallet.

4.11.03
Luke 21:19: "In your patience possess ye your souls."

19

Get Back Up Again

~

Get back up again:
That is what the singer sang on TV.
I thought to myself, "It is true."
My voice may be under medication,
And my body may be yelling, too,
But my spirit is saying,
"Jesus, I love You.
Jesus, I worship You.
Jesus, I praise You.

Jesus, I give you glory
For encouraging me.
For lifting me up,
For giving me hope,
For giving me breath.
Jesus, You are the answer.
You lift me like no other.
You are my reason for living.

You are the life within me.
You are the love within me.
You are the joy within me.
You are the peace within me.
You are my best friend.
You are my Lord and Savior.
Thanks…for loving me
Soooooooooooo *much*!" ☺

4.13.03
Psalms 150:6: "Let every thing that hath breath praise the Lord. Praise ye the Lord!"

20

A Tear-Mingled Shower

~⌀

The drops of water from the shower
Mingled with my tears.
God knew why I cried.
Emotions are given for a reason.
Recently it seems I have a lot of emotions.
To be honest, maybe I should say—
To be transparent, I must say—
When you have been diagnosed with cancer
And are recovering from surgery,
As you lie in that bed
Day after day, week after week,
Fighting germs and viruses
On top of the recent diagnosis,
Before long you realize
You don't care if you shower or not,
Let alone fix your hair and makeup.
You don't even care enough to use lotion.

As for cologne, why bother?
There is no purpose.

I see others who have been very kind to me
Building their homes daily,
Mowing the grass and trimming,
Rearranging furniture,
Raising children...I'm happy for them.
I feel like a bystander
Because I can't participate.
It makes me feel useless,
Yet I know that is not true.
I am in the very early stages
Of learning about cancer.

If this is all there is to life,
It is merely existing, and who would want that?
How can I look ahead and keep my chin up?
As I prepare to move to Canada,
I look forward to spending time with family,

But I pray I do not feel like an observer.
It will never be the same
As having my own home,
Yet I need to be somewhere.
Surely God has a place for me
To fit, to be a blessing.
He knows the end from the beginning
I'm believing in Romans 8:28.
I am also learning how to bless
Someone else who is ill.
Give her a free pedicure,
Watch her get up and about,

Give her a coupon to get her nails done
Or a fresh haircut (if she has any—some do keep it).
Let her know you care.
Phone her even if it is long distance,
Phone her when it isn't long distance, too.
She needs a hug as well—lots.
There is a lot you can do.
She is not sick because she wants to be.
TV does not remove her pain.

I know because I am talking from my transparent heart—
Telling it like it is.
So maybe you can help someone
Want to look forward to another day;
Just look into his or her eyes

And release the love God has given you.
Love never fails.

4.12.03
1 Corinthians 13:4–8: "Charity suffereth long, and is kind; charity envieth not; charity vaunteth not itself, is not puffed up, Doth not behave itself unseemly, seeketh not her own, is not easily provoked, thinketh no evil; Rejoiceth not in iniquity, but rejoiceth in the truth; Beareth all things, believeth all things, hopeth all things, endureth all things. Charity never faileth: but whether there be prophecies they shall fail; whether there be tongues, they shall cease; whether there be knowledge, it shall vanish away."

21

Closing the Gap

~

As I prepared to publish this book, I made a discovery.
There was a defining moment I was not able to write
about before.
I will now attempt to fill you in because the memory
Has been etched in my mind
Like a tattoo since I walked through the door.

The door was to the office of the oncologist,
Whose wife entered first.
I was excited and told her why.
In one more day, as my son had purchased the plane ticket,
I was going to be able to fly
Back to Canada, where my family was waiting.
I had been doing a countdown as each day passed by.
Suddenly she left the office,
But I did not know why.
Then both she and her husband came in.
We sat, and he told me
They'd found a tumor with the scan.
I thought it meant another surgery.

I was in a lot of pain still,
And the thought of being opened up again
Was almost overwhelming…
So much pain…

He assured me,
No, no more surgery.
That was an instant relief.
Then he said I'd have to take radiation and chemotherapy!

What could I do?
I knew God showed me not to do so,
But this was a whole new ball game.
I could not say no.

Thinking I would fly back home
And get the treatments in Toronto,
I decided it would be good to be near family,
So I'd just do it when I went.
That was not what he said.
I needed to start immediately
Because it was a fast-growing type of cancer.
I could not fly; he grounded me.

The shock was so severe.
To fly home was what I longed for.
It was what I'd looked forward to
Ever since the surgery several weeks before.

Then he told me the chemotherapy treatments
Would be three weeks apart.
When we calculated, it meant staying five months more.
It broke my heart.

That meant being in Texas in the hot summer weather
From April until the end of August, approximately.
Yet I could not sit in the sun and enjoy it at all.
This was all kicking in; it was reality.

Radiation was needed, too.
Twenty-eight treatments in all—five each week.
I had not even considered the possibility.
I could not speak.

As just three weeks prior to surgery
I received insurance coverage, I knew that was why
I must stay and do this, so there was no decision to make.
The cost would be $50,000.

Next came the moment of severest intensity
Because the tumor was at the top of my lung,
Near my larynx...I said, "Will I lose my voice?"
There was a long deathly silence...I thought I would
crack...
Then the nurse said, "Do you sing?"
I kept looking at the doctor and answered her, "Yes."
I was discerning whether the doctor would tell the truth
And knew her question gave him more time to answer.

He had tears in his eyes and said, "No."
Although I was not totally convinced,
Some pressure lifted, and I said:
"What do I do?"

In my heart I knew crying would not change a thing.
I needed to see past the problem.
My prayer had been for God to show me
His path to my healing, and I saw it.

God uses doctors, nurses, medicine, chemotherapy,
Radiation—all of the above and much more.
Had people not been praying previously,
I'd be dead now, so God did not let me down.

He said He would see me through, and I believed it.
My next question was if I would lose my hair.
He pointed to my long ponytail and said
It would not be as long.

He was kind of breaking the news gently,
So I let him know there was a clip attached,
And my hair was not all that long, but it was past my shoulders.
We all laughed, and it broke the tension a bit...a lot, in fact.

Then I wondered about the refund on the plane ticket.
As it turned out, there was no problem.
When it is a case such as this, they oblige.
So I was glad for my son—yet another problem solved.

I walked through the waiting room,
Where there were many people.
I felt like a zombie as my feet kept on stepping through.
When I got to the parking lot, I started to shake.

As I sat in my pickup truck, the tears wouldn't release.
My arms shook, and I realized in my heart was peace.
I almost did not want it to be there
Because all was *not* well; yet it was there.

I thought to myself, ***"This is when I need a friend with me."***
It was the most alone I'd ever felt in my life,
Yet as I prayed, in just moments I knew
My best Friend was with me...Jesus.

It was at a time like this that any price I'd had to
pay previously
For not compromising in my Christian walk
Was nothing to fret about at all.
Because as I sat, Jesus began to talk.

We had a relationship that did not begin on this day.
My roots had grown deep over the past twenty-five years.
Though I needed to study the Word more,
I was in communion with Him daily and overcame
many fears.

He said, **"I know it looks like I've let you down,
but I haven't."**
He reminded me that He would see me through.

I just didn't know the valley would be so deep.
Facing it head on was the only thing to do.

I had a goal to return to Canada and my family,
Yet my flesh did not want to face the mountains.
Sometimes we get thrown a curveball.
Sometimes a detour is what is needed, but it is
not a dead end.

I drove down the road, bravely wiping away a few tears
As a new chapter of my life began.
I thought about my dad, who had died of cancer (lymph
nodes), and
Rejoiced that he'd been saved before the end—

The same regarding my cousin who died young.
Suddenly any gap between heaven and earth closed.
I felt close to loved ones and friends that had passed on.
However, I had no fear and knew it was not my time.

This was definitely not a time to go into denial.
So I faced the fear, determined to overcome.
It was difficult phoning my family sixteen hundred
miles away.
They were disappointed but glad I have a survivor mentality.

My son said, *"Mom, you're tough; you're Canadian!"*
It is amazing how so few words can spark your
plugs encouragingly.
When the going got tough, those were the kinds of words
That came back to help me.

My daughter phoned regularly, and I phoned her.
We laughed together at times and cried together, too.
My brother and sister-in-law called me,
And a few friends from Canada called occasionally.
A hug by phone is better than none at all.
Yet phones are somehow not regarded that way,
Sad to say.
I trust you now know why
I couldn't write about this before.
In retrospect, I'm just so grateful.
I knew Jesus escorted me out that door.

10.30.07
Proverbs 18:24: "A man that hath friends must shew himself friendly: and there is a friend that sticketh closer than a brother."

22

Day-Surgery Trauma

~~~

THIS IS ONE of the events I could not write about when it happened. The eight-inch incision in my side and back was healed enough after several weeks to enable chemotherapy treatments to begin. (There were no sutures. A glue-like substance held me together! When I was told, it made me kind of not want to stretch, let alone sneeze!)

Prior to beginning chemotherapy treatments, I was admitted to the hospital for day surgery to have the main line inserted. (Day surgery means the patient is expected to return home the same day.) An opening is made, and then a small, sharp, straw-like tube (not a real needle) is inserted and pushed into position toward the heart. The exposed end is close to where my bra strap goes, and this is where future needles will be inserted rather than in my body. It is a wonderful invention. I expected to be done and out of there in an hour or two. Wrong!

The doctor who did the procedure was the same doctor who did my lung surgery, so I was very glad. (Since the initial surgery, I had been on pain pills, and as it turned out, I was on them for five months. Thankfully there was no addiction whatsoever.) As I entered the day-surgery area, there were about twelve spots for people to lie on stretchers in little areas closed in by cloth curtains. This meant we could all hear each other. A male nurse and my doctor stood by me, and there was no more room for anyone to enter.

After opening the kit, treating me, and waiting the appropriate time for the area to become numb, they began the day surgery. There was only one problem: the area was *not numb*...and I let the doctor know it! A second kit was brought in. Now I had a double dose of numbing. Once again, the doctor started, and it was so painful! I tried not to scream because I did not want to frighten the other patients. I figured they had their own battles, and I was trying to be thoughtful. I bit the sheet and my knuckles and groaned, and then I heard the doctor say, "What kind of drugs are you taking?"

I said, "Only what you prescribed!" I was shocked and started to get angry, but I certainly was not in any position to confront anyone.

The next thing I heard was a woman's voice: "Need some help in here?" Then I felt her hands hold my ankles down—not good, because that made me think she knew the area was not going to freeze. Then another nurse came and stood by the other side, doing the same thing. They became the wall instead of the curtain. I tried to relax because I did not want to move away from where the doctor was making the incision, but it still hurt so badly that I said out loud, "Oh Lord, help me...don't let me faint..." Then it was like a light came on, and I prayed, "Lord, yes...*let* me faint!"

It may sound funny now, but it wasn't then, because I did *not* faint. I had to tough it out. I could hardly believe it was happening because it was extremely stressful and painful, as well as frustrating for the doctor also. There was a lot of groaning, and it was definitely *not* my best day. Incredibly, I just knew other patients were praying for me, asking God to help me, and it touched my heart. The Holy Spirit has ways of revealing things like this, and He did. I was exhausted afterward and so glad when the doctor was done.

Everyone left except one male nurse, who dressed the incision area. When he was done, I started to cry with relief because it was over. He had so much compassion and knew exactly what to do. **We hooked pinky fingers on one hand, and that is all he did, without speaking one word, but he refused to leave when a nurse called him elsewhere.** As I wiped tears away with my other hand, he waited patiently until my tears were released. His act of compassion was a huge step in my healing process. I was able to release all the stress.

Then he turned to leave, and I simply said, "Thank you." He had tears in his eyes as he looked over his shoulder at my face and nodded to me. It was a special moment, and I believe that is exactly what Jesus would have done if it would have been Jesus in that physical body helping me! Sometimes it is so easy to help in a big way, yet it is also very easy to miss the opportunity. Thankfully, he did not leave when someone called him out. **After all, he was working—working compassion.**

Now that everyone had left my little space, I sat up to get dressed. I could hardly wait to get out of there. As I stood up and turned, I almost fainted. I was not prepared to see all that blood on the sheet where I had been lying. It alarmed me. Nevertheless, I got dressed and got out of there. Partway out, as I was feeling very shaky, someone came with a wheelchair and escorted me to the exit. I am certain that for most people, this is not such an ordeal, but in my case, it was.

As wonderful as it was to be able to use the main line in the future, it also was creating problems. My bra strap was directly in line with the attachment, and it was necessary to avoid disturbing it.

Also, the plastic apparatus could be seen easily no matter what blouse I wore, and a T-shirt would rub against it, so that did not work. I kept trying something else and finally decided it did not matter if someone saw the apparatus. What mattered was that I was getting the help I needed. It's not like I could keep the cancer a secret, as I expected to be bald two weeks after the first chemo treatment. Yet at the time, I was facing the mountains one step at a time, and I did not yet see the big picture. It is simply called *coping*.

When you are facing cancer, staying focused is not easy, because there are so many bends in the road. Aggravation tried to loom up every time I got dressed because nothing worked. Also, I started thinking everyone would be looking at that tube, and I did not want to talk about the cancer. I just needed to get through it. Talking about it did not change the diagnosis. In reality, most people are so caught up in their own problems that few have time to worry about your concerns. I needed to turn from aggravation to appreciation, and I did.

The day the main line was removed truly was my graduation day—not the last chemo treatment or the last radiation treatment; it was when the main line was removed. I paid my dues to celebrate that victory! Now that small scar is a reminder of another valley the Lord brought me through. Also, the scar became a reminder to look for opportunities to show compassion to others.

For the benefit of anyone facing a main line soon, I can honestly tell you that of all the patients I saw in that six-month time frame, not one other patient had a problem with his or her main line—only me. Why me? Who knows! **Goliath was conquered, that is all that matters. Glory to God!**

Romans 8:37: "Nay, in all these things we are more than conquerors through him that loved us."

23

My Reason for Living

I don't much want to watch TV.
Now I know why.
When I see a man look lovingly
Into a woman's eyes
And reach out to embrace her,
It seems a dream that passed me by.
So who needs to be reminded of that...?
Certainly not me.
I forgave.
I try to look ahead,
Yet it seems everything I see
Has somehow escaped me.
No sense in forming a list;
I lost everything
Except Jesus!
Somehow, I sense an expectancy
Of what those five words really mean.
I can expect that Jesus is enough
Because I did not deny Him
Even when I lost everything.
It was only Jesus who was there all the time.
I did not have to panic and run looking for Him.

He was within me,
Closer to me than the problems.
He comforted and encouraged me.
He carried me when necessary.
He lovingly led me up higher and higher
From one mountaintop to another
Until the circumstances did not matter,
For I was lost in love—His love.
His love enveloped me from head to toe.

His loving presence is with me
Everywhere I go.
He is my reason for living.

4.12.03
1 John 3:2–3: "Beloved, now are we the sons of God, and it doth not yet appear what we shall be: but we know that, when he shall appear, we shall be like him; for we shall see him as he is. And every man that hath this hope in him purifieth himself, even as he is pure.

24

What Would You Do?

~

It may sound funny when read,
But I feel like I'm the only person
In the whole world
Who is awake at 2:00 a.m.
On a Saturday night,
And I am not impressed.
A person can only sleep so much.
A person can only pray so much.
A person who is trying to keep herself encouraged
Can find her eyes on herself too much
When it comes to this.
So what do I do?
Lie low so as not to disturb other people
In the household.
Can't go for a walk
And look at the moon and stars:
Everyone's dog would bark for sure.
I could pray quietly.

Read the Word.
Try to go to sleep.
Listen to the Lord.
At least I know He doesn't sleep.
He's at the right hand of the Father,
Praying for you and me.
I could also be appreciative of the fact
That I usually sleep very well every night,
So I pray for everyone who has had surgery
And everyone who is facing surgery.
I pray for the president, all leaders, and the troops—
Their families too.
Next thing I know, my eyes open, and it is morning.
So, if you can't sleep, now you know what to do too!

4.13.03
1 Thessalonians 5:17: "Pray without ceasing."

25

Just a Breath Away

~

The CD kept turning.
Music filled the living room.
Heartstrings were pulled.
My ears became fine tuned
As the voices sang in harmony.
Lyrics of truth and inspiration
Poured forth spontaneously.
I could not move from my chair.
The Spirit of the Lord was all over me.
Tears fell as He touched me
Time and again.
I knew what my Lord and Savior
Was saying to me without a doubt:
"I am just a breath away."
That is very encouraging
To someone with lung cancer
Recovering from surgery
And facing radiation and chemo.
I was reminded the Father hears
Through the silence and the tears.
The more I listened,
The more God blessed me.

One little anointed song
Encouraged me to pray—
Pray no matter what I face,
Pray to go on believing.
No wonder God wants me to praise Him.
He is uplifted, and so am I.
Praise the Lord.
As the Word says,
"Let everything that has breath
Praise the Lord!"
That is me, because I have breath.
Praise the Lord!

4.19.03
Isaiah 40:31: "But they that wait upon the Lord shall renew their strength; they shall mount up with wings as eagles; they shall run, and not be weary; and they shall walk, and not faint."

26

At the Foot of the Cross

~⌒

Michael W. Smith won a Dove award.
He referred to it as

"Another thing to lay at the foot of the Cross
As I cannot take it with me."

My heart was touched by his humility.
I felt tears come as I said,
"Lord, what do I have to lay at the cross?
I have no awards or trophies or plaques.
I do give You my will,
Yet I want to give so much more.
I give You my manuscripts,
My poems, and my songs."
Yet it seems unjust
As the manuscripts aren't published,
And the songs are unsung,
At least at this point in time.
Yet I never want to give You
A half-baked cake
Or a baked cake that is not iced.
So, help me, Jesus,

To somehow complete
What I have begun
Because I want to honor You, Lord.
I want to please You.
I want to fulfill my calling,
Though I may never win a Dove award.
My prayer is that my songs
Will somehow touch millions of hearts—
My books and poems, too.

Only You know how to make it happen.
I commit them to You, God.
Thy will be done,
In Jesus's name. Amen.

4.26.03
Proverbs 16:3: "Commit thy works unto the Lord, and thy thoughts shall be established."

27

Brother Breaks Through

My brother, sister-in-law, and I
Were talking on the phone together.
We had a good visit.
Then something happened
That has never, ever happened
In over fifty years.
My brother told me he loved me!
I was speechless!
My sister-in-law piped up, "Bye, Linda,"
And I could "hear" her smiling...
I said, "Bye,"
Hung up the phone,
And felt ten feet tall
As my spirit soared in ecstasy.
It was a moment I will never forget.
It was a breakthrough—
A complete breakthrough!

Then I thought back to my childhood years.
Bobby and I knew our parents loved us,
But it was not because Daddy said it.
He never once told us he loved us.

He showed it in his actions
But did not take the liberty to speak those words.
He had never heard them from his father, either.
Knowing this helps me realize
What a major breakthrough this is.
It has been broken after many generations.
I praise God and give Him glory.
I am not sure whom
I am happier for:
Bobby or me.
But I sure am
Happy! ☺

4.28.03
Isaiah 58:6: "...that you break every yoke..."

28

A Crappy Day

The world would say, "That sucks!"
I say, "It's a crappy day!"
I believed to *keep* my hair.
Not so…
Life is *not* fair!
I know God will give me peace,
See me through,
But…(I know: no buts
Because they are followed by a negative)
But…what is happening to my *faith*?
I am very concerned.
I believed I was healed.
I believed the tumor would be gone
Before surgery.
It was still there.
I believed to keep my hair.
Not so.
It is falling out by the handful today.
Yeah, another red-letter day,
May 9, 2003: Friday!
So, the hairdresser will shave it off
At 8:00 p.m.

I did cut it much shorter, just in case,
But now it means no more cute pixie cut—
No more nothing.

It hurts.
I try not to let emotions rule.
The Lord has been preparing me.
My flesh just does not *want*
To go through this.
It means no hair from May through December.
Who could get excited about that—
Male or female?
I put a black terry-cloth turban
In my purse in preparation.
That's all I *can do.*
"I can do all things through Christ
Who strengthens me."
So
I lean on You, Lord.
I draw strength from You.
I ask You to help me
To turn this day around
From a "crappy day"
To a Christ-centered day.
I have to be transparent
And write what I live.
I am being honest
And doing my best.
I ask You to anoint what I do
And do the rest...
I claim Romans 8:28.

There seem to be so many, many mountains
That I have had to climb
In the last three years.
I do not quit or give up,
But there *is* a limit, Lord,
To what I can stand.
I am not infallible, you know.
How about lifting me up
To the very top
Of the next huge mountain
As we soar like eagles together?
Because You said You would give me
The desires of my heart
If I delighted myself in You.
I desire to be able to *skip*
The agony of climbing the next mountain
And have You lift me to the top
As together we shine brilliantly.
Jesus, please…please…
It is time for a breakthrough!

5.9.03
Philippians 4:13: "I can do all things through Christ which strengtheneth me."

29

You Bet

~~

Things are just happening too fast!
My hair started falling out this morning.
I tried to prepare myself for getting my head shaved at eight.
Even though, in preparation,
I had been getting my hair cut shorter gradually,
My emotions were in turmoil.
I couldn't cry; it wouldn't change anything anyway.
Trying to picture myself bald was not easy.
My purse had no money for a wig.
Thank God for the two turbans a friend bought me.
Then my daughter phoned this afternoon.
She was very concerned about Mom.
I told her I'd be okay—
Admitted I felt some anger and
Was trying to deal with it.
UPS arrived with a parcel for me.
It was totally unexpected:
Three boxes of assorted chocolates
From my son, daughter-in-law, and two grandsons.
Then the mailman arrived
With a homemade Mother's Day card.
Another friend and her daughters had made it:

Beautiful roses and a lace-trimmed poem.
I felt God loving me
Through family and friends
From sixteen hundred miles away.
A phone call, a UPS delivery, and a mail delivery
Arriving simultaneously:

Does God know how to deliver or what?
Does God have perfect timing?
Does God know how to get my attention?

You bet!

5.10.03
James 1:17: "Every good gift and every perfect gift is from above, and cometh down from the Father of lights, with whom is no variableness, neither shadow of turning."

30

Close Shave

~

In one hour, my head gets shaved.
God, help me please.
Prepare me, give me grace.
Strengthen my emotions
So they don't rule.
I must trust You in everything.
Help me, Lord.
If I were one of those people
Who let her hair go scraggly,
This would be no big deal.
I have always tried to look after my hair—
Wear it different ways,
Enjoy using clips and bows and flowers.
Maybe that is why now,
When I think about having
A bald head,
I feel ashamed.
The thought makes me want to hide,
But I can't.
Life goes on.
Besides, my hair will grow again,
Someday, some month—

Hopefully this year.
Meanwhile,
I am watching
World's Funniest Videos
Because I want to laugh again.
I just can't lose my merry heart.

Help me, Jesus.
Hold me close...
Because this...
Is
Not
Funny!

5.9.03
Proverbs 17:22: "A merry heart doeth good like a medicine: but a broken spirit drieth the bones."

31

A Short Visit with Number One

~⌒

Next, the visit to the hairdresser.
In just minutes
She shaved my head.
I managed to look in the mirror—
Saw a golden glow...
This wise hairdresser knew better
Than to shave my head absolutely bald.
It would have been stark white and very slippery.
She put the power clippers on number one.
I put on my black terry-cloth turban,
Held my chin up, and took a big breath—
Looked at the hair on the floor and
Was surprised there was that much.
Then I heard the hairdresser say
She had three good wigs that were her mother's.
One was golden blond, one was ash blond,
And one was frosted.

My heart was moved when I heard the colors.
She then said, "I want you to have them."

Does my God supply my needs?
Does my God know how to come through?
Does my God have perfect timing?
Does my God know I spent my last $3.50 on gas?
Does my God know I learned to be content
With a lot and with a little?
Does my God answer my prayers…?
My emotions were not in control.
Christ in me, the hope of glory,
Gave me the peace that passes all understanding, and
Taught me to trust Him in every situation.

The more I walk in peace and in love,
The more I see Jesus revealing Himself to me.
My short visit with number one
Had once again
Turned out to be fun!
God does know
How to turn things around for good! ☺

5.10.03
Philippians 4:19: "But my God shall supply all your need according to his riches in glory by Christ Jesus."

32

An Unfinished Work

~⌣

On went the hot-pink nightcap.
I laid my head on my pillow,
Surprised that my scalp hurt.
It was tender and sore to touch.
Chemo does strange things sometimes.
It kills cancer yet hurts your scalp.
I wondered how long the discomfort would last.
Then the nightcap felt too warm,
Yet I definitely did not want to be seen,
So, I left it on.
I also left the poem
Unfinished…

Psalms 147:3 "He healeth the broken in heart, and bindeth up their wounds."

33

Patient Cancer Patient

Help me, Lord, to tell others
What it is like to have cancer
So they will have compassion
For those You want them to love
As Your compassion (not pity)
Flows through them to help others in need.
Although I have peace,
There is anger stirring within.
I'm conscious of it,
Don't like it,
Am not sure why it is there.
But I have to *deal with it*!

As I search my heart
With the help of the Holy Spirit,
I am quickly reminded of much:
A lot of major things I prayed about
Have crumbled rapidly before my eyes
Circumstances are the complete reverse
Of what I prayed and confessed and stood on the Word for.
No wonder I am concerned about what is happening
To my faith…

Is it wavering or growing?
Is there doubt or fervent expectancy?
Am I angry at God
Even though I know He loves me and
Wants the best for me?
That is why He sent His Son.
I know the thief is the devil.
I know sickness comes from him.
Yet...in my heart, I hear a voice saying,
"But he can't do anything God does not allow..."
That voice would make me angry at God.

So something is wrong
Because no one ever wins an argument with God.
He's never lost at anything.
He only knows victory.
He did not lose His Son,
He *gave* His Son (John 3:16).
There is a difference!
Knowing this helps me realize
This anger is rooted in fear...
What am I afraid of?
Ponder...
Maybe I should ask myself,
"What am I believing in?"
Total healing, wholeness, restoration of everything—
Relationships, finances, material things—
Christian marriage that glorifies God—
Books to be published, songs, poems...
Yes, I am believing in God for all of this and more.
Because He is able to do far exceedingly above

All I ever hope, think, or ask for.
Even though I suffered a shipwreck, so to speak,
God restores...
So, what's the problem?

Could it be I need to be more patient as I wait on
God's timing?
After all, harvest time always comes.
I've sent my ship out
With decades of tithing and offerings,
So, I have no doubt my harvest
Has not all come in yet.
Am I afraid of dying?
No, not at all.
In fact, I hardly think about death,
Because I choose life.
I choose to believe
I shall live and not die.

So I am seeking God daily
As to His will for me.
The more I experience,
The more I have to write about.
It is that simple.
So why the anger, and is there fear?
Could it be that the real me,
The spirit man on the inside,
Feels like a prisoner?
How so?

Because regardless of how much I enjoy life,
I can't get away from the cancer
That is inside my body.
It seems to imprison me,
Though it is unseen,
Because of the present restrictions—
Such as not sitting in the direct sun
When it is May 10 in Amarillo, Texas.
Losing my hair, having difficulty in swallowing—
It feels like a cracker is stuck in my throat.
My strength does not last all day;
I need to lie down and rest.
Short walks leave me short of breath.
My appetite is not what it should be.
Joints are sore at times,
And I have got five more chemo treatments to go.
No wonder I feel like a prisoner:
One ugly diagnosis of lung cancer,
And my life is in a whirlwind.

For twenty days each month (for two months),
I have twenty radiation treatments,
One chemo every three weeks,
Four doctor appointments, and
Four hospital visits to draw blood and change dressings.
That is twenty-nine trips to the doctor in twenty days:
A lot for a healthy person to cope with!

Yet as the Holy Spirit imparts wisdom,
I see another viewpoint

So vital to capturing the big picture!
Closer to me than the cancer,
Closer to me than the circumstances,
Closer to me than every problem
Is Jesus…on the inside:
Jesus in my heart,
Jesus in my soul (mind, will, emotions),
Jesus in my life—
And not just for a visit…
He dwells in me.
My heart is his home.
So why all the fussing?

It is Jesus who paid the price
For me to have peace in the midst of the storm—
For me to be able to smile and have joy, too—
For me to be optimistic through it all.
Because it is Jesus
Who said He'd see me through,
And He never lets me down.

It is because of Jesus
I press on with my chin up and shoulders back.
It is because of Jesus
And knowing Him intimately
That I can shine and be clamorously foolish
Because I know the circumstances
Are subject to change.
As I speak the things that are not
As though they were,
As I stand on the promises of God,

As I continue to be obedient,
As I continue to pray,
It is well with my soul!
It really is—
Because God is in charge.
Perfect love casts out all fear.
God reveals Himself to me many times
And in many ways each day.
He *is* seeing me through this valley.
He *is* walking beside me each step of the way.
Progress *is* being made daily.
I *really am* okay.

That doesn't mean I do not need help, though.
I do, and God uses people.
I need hugs; I need phone calls.
I need visits, a card, a letter, a flower;
I need a laugh, a cry, a new memory to cherish;
An encouraging word, a scripture for sure,
An invitation to dinner, fellowship.
How about a pedicure for a treat?
Or a gift certificate to make long-distance phone calls?
A manicure, a guitar lesson,
Some homemade cookies,
A drive in the country,
A new praise and worship CD...?
See, there are lots of things a person can do,
And it need not cost money, either.
When you can just be you,
God can use you mightily
Because *you* won't be in the way.

It will be God's love pouring through you:
Touching, healing, encouraging,
Comforting, uplifting, strengthening
As only God can do!
I pray what I have just written
Encourages you to be you
And let God do
What He wants to do

Because His plan for your life is good.
In fact, it is great.
So be sure to "occupy till He comes"
Because there is much to do.
Let Him flow like a river through you.
Stay pure, holy, undefiled.
Take the limits off.
Lean not on your own understanding;
Just let Him do what He wants to do.
He is not through blessing you!

5.10.03
**Romans 12:12: "Rejoicing in hope; patient in tribulation;
continuing instant in prayer;"**

34

My Praise Report to Friends

~

FYI: Excerpts of a letter written two months after surgery, showing my mind-set:

05.11.03
Dear [seven names],
When the chemo and radiation treatments are done, it will be August. Two weeks after the last chemo treatment, I will be coming back home to live. Hopefully, there will be no complications or delays. So far so good. I was not sick at all after the first chemo, so they have made a lot of improvements in the medicine. I am sooooo glad, because I do NOT like to throw up! ☺

The weather is beautiful, high 70s and 80s now, grass real green and all the leaves are out. Not me though, as I am not to sit in the direct sun so that is a bit of a challenge. I use the big swing in the morning before the sun shines in the back yard. Then in the afternoon I can sit at the front of the house as there is a wide overhang to protect. I use my computer quite a bit to write...I have manuscripts in my briefcase to bring home and I WILL be an AUTHOR someday, praise God!

The family I am living with blessed me with the master bedroom and bathroom and it is very convenient. Mirrors on the closet doors and ceiling fan, central air, and I have my little television.

The doctors are pleased with my progress, and cannot understand why my throat is NOT really sore...or why I'm NOT having trouble swallowing food and water (because of the radiation in the upper lung area). I told the doctor a lot of people are praying for me. He said, "There's nothing wrong with that!" Praise God I found a doctor that recognizes he has limitations but God doesn't. ☺

The next chemo treatment is this week, then another one three weeks later. Pray my blood pressure stays stable during the treatment so there are no complications. I need six chemo treatments in all, every three weeks. One of my friends stayed with me for moral support for a lot of that time and it helped.

I am working on a book to help others see the viewpoint of a cancer survivor. I have learned a lot, especially the importance of having compassion. Religious spirits do not help at all, nor do dogmatic people who mean well, but are not walking in love. As always, Jesus is our example and if anyone knows anything about compassion, He is the Master of compassion. I feel His presence continually and He has miraculously helped me to be strong and at peace as He walks me through this incredible valley, but WE WILL...come through victoriously.

He said He would be with me every step of the way, it would not be easy, and that He would see me through. I wanted to hear something different, like I will receive the manifestation of the healing in a week, or whatever, but that is not what He said.

Nevertheless, in the most difficult times He reminds me of the Rhema word He gave me, and I am totally at peace and able to rest in Him and trust Him completely. Jesus truly is the answer...that is all there is to it! I pray each of you are continually drawing closer to Him and enjoying His presence.

The two-year-old girl where I live calls me **Lala**...for Linda. My youngest grandson in Canada calls me **Grammie TAAAAAXXAS! I love it!** ☺

I did lose my hair on Friday, but it will grow back, maybe by December or January. It was kind of fun to retire my blow dryer, curling irons, brush, combs, electric razor, etc. What a time saver eh?! See, God can have GOOD come out of anything! (That does not mean I do not have to make any adjustments, it is difficult but He is giving me grace.) Besides, the turbans are pretty nice. Yesterday I was given a bag with ten, yes TEN...wigs...and another lady promised me three wigs. Praise the Lord. (Now for the right color...) ☺ Decisions, decisions...

God really supplies all my needs. In case you did not know I am totally dependent on the Lord and He is really looking after me. I answered His call and He has given me lots to write about as He continues to prove Himself faithful. He even looked after all the $50,000.00 bill for chemo and radiation. My God is a debt canceling God! Makes me glad I did not ever stop tithing or sowing offerings in the last twenty-four years as a Christian. When you have sent the ship out, you have faith for the harvest to come in when it is needed! ☺

My friend Donna, where I live, had a **$25,000.00 medical bill canceled this week when one of her daughters was in intensive care over a week in January. God saved** her life, there was no brain or heart damage, and He also took care of the finances. **God knows how to look after details.** Oh to trust Him more…She helped me so much, and God helped her right back where she needed it most. Hallelujah!

Chin up everyone, keep praying please, and I will see y'all soon. Much love, and hope this lengthy letter helps make up for the other times when I wanted to write but was not up to it. I am with you in spirit though, praise God…

Lovingly, Linda.

Galatians 6:9: "And let us not be weary in well doing: for in due season we shall reap, if we faint not."

35

Seeking God's Face

God, Your Word states clearly
You want me to prosper and be in health
As my soul prospers.
Last year I thought I received excellent teaching,
Attended church three times per week faithfully,
Applied the teaching to my life—
While simultaneously within my lung
A tumor was growing larger and larger.
Help me to understand, Lord.
I come to You, I seek Your face, not man's.
As I was employed at that time
And did my job as unto You...
Help me understand...
In hindsight, yes, I see Romans 8:28.

You uprooted me to protect me from backbiters
And carnal Christians
Because you knew the mountain I would face.
You planted me elsewhere.
I knew but two in the new congregation,
Yet you provided the help I needed.
When the people you have hand-chosen

To be of assistance to me
Are led by the Holy Spirit,
It does not require a crowd.
You put me in contact
With a family who is also
Climbing a steep mountain.
Consequently, we can relate to each other,
Encourage each other,
Bless each other,
Lift up each other's hands.
Why?
Because You are faithful.
You have a plan.
You are in my life to stay.
It is as simple as that.

5.12.03
1 Corinthians 1:9: "God is faithful by whom ye were called unto the fellowship of his Son Jesus Christ our Lord."

36

Lovin' on God

~

When your body needs to rest
As you fight the flu…whatever else,
Your mind has lots of time to think.
That is good though, really good,
Because everyone needs to learn
How to be still before God—
Simply bask in His presence,
Simply soak up that love like a sponge.
Yet it is so easy to be so busy—
As His face we cannot see—
That we hurry and scurry about repeatedly.
Then suddenly another day is gone,
And we've not stepped off life's treadmill
Long enough to love on God for a while,
To praise and thank Him for His faithfulness,
To acknowledge His presence in our lives,
His hand of intervention, the leading of the Holy Spirit,
The wisdom and understanding He gives,
The comfort in the midst of it all,
Not to mention the answers we need
To so many questions that surface.

He's there all the time, waiting patiently.
So why don't we put him first
And receive what we need so our "sponge" is not dry?
We'd be pliable and much more effective.
Could it be we don't trust Him enough?
Could it be we want to hold the reins of control…
Maybe just a little bit?
Are our egos being fed?
If we are being Spirit-led
Maybe more lights would come on
As we speak forth words of life
Inspired by the Holy Spirit.
As we look up, we know God's looking down,
Wanting to reveal more to us.
So, let's head for our secret place and
Be willing to lie before the Master,
Who will mold these clay vessels
Into something beautiful He can use
As we become more Christlike daily,
As we are continually being changed
Into His image as our minds are transformed
By the Word of God, and our hearts are full of love.
We can't stay where we are.
We must keep climbing up spiritually,
Pressing in to the heart of God and pressing on
Even from a bed of affliction—but that is okay.
This too shall pass, and we will come forth
As purified gold, vessels to behold.
It is God's plan.

5.13.03
Job 23:10: "But he knoweth the way that I take: when he has tested me, I shall come forth as gold."

37

God's Love in Action

~∿

The red velvet petals on a rose
Hug each other.
Together
They make something beautiful.

Each one is significant.
Each one has a job to do
Individually and collectively.
They cannot be replaced,
Nor can you.

Like the petals on the rose,
You are necessary.
You have a job to do.
You are part of what makes that rose
Something beautiful.

Your love is the food that makes it grow.
Your compassion heals the wounds.
Your prayers keep it alive.
You are God's love in action.
Yes, you

Are God's love
In
Action!

(Song lyrics llj)
//

38

Chapters Closing

~~

One phone call was made.
After conversing with my friend,
I realized my relationship with her
Was like a chapter of my life closing.
God is leading me to Canada.
A transition is taking place.
My spirit was troubled.
It felt like I was dropping off the earth—
As if I was so insignificant
No one would even miss me.
I'd be like a fading, wilted rose,
Once radiant and full of life,
Suddenly conscious of every breath,
Wanting to believe there is a purpose
In me moving back to Canada.
Not that I'm going back there to die—
Yet where is purpose for my life?
No matter how many days I have,
No matter how many months or years,

What am I here for?
What can I do?
Bond with family and grandchildren, yes.
Yet each day I need a reason to live.
Forgive me Lord, at my age, for
Asking this, yet I need Your help.
I do not want to be alone, yet I am not sure
If Your plan means I stay single or not.
I do not want to be a burden to my family,
Yet I do not want to live alone.
I did that most of my life,
Even when married I was alone much
Like an abandoned wife.

Yet people need people, and I'm no exception.
I do want my books published.
Maybe...oh...just help me, please, Lord.

Give me a vision for the future,
Your plan for my life:
Purpose.
In Jesus's name, I pray.
Amen.

5.14.03
Jeremiah 29:11: "For I know the thoughts that I think toward you, saith the Lord, thoughts of peace and not of evil, to give you an expected end."

39

I Need to Tell You Something

~~

**Not just because of a cancer diagnosis I
received recently;
It is because I don't want anyone's blood on my hands.
I need to tell everyone something:**

Jesus is the only bridge to heaven.
Just because I was diagnosed with cancer
Does not mean I'll die before friends and family.
No one knows his or her appointed time;
One just relates cancer with death
Then assumes I'm likely to be the next one.
Not necessarily true…
And *that*…is a *fact!*
Consequently, I feel it is my duty
To tell each of you, in love, what is in my heart.

Please serve Jesus with your whole heart.
Please give Him first place in your life.
Life on earth is so short for each of us
In relation to eternity…
We'll have eternity to be together.
Nothing you do for Jesus will ever be wasted.

Do what you do as unto Him.
He honors obedience.
His plan is so good.
He has not overlooked you.
He will never abandon you.
You can walk away from Him…
Please don't…stay close to His heart.
He loves you more than you'll ever know.

How do I know?
The Bible tells me so.
Little ones to him belong.
They are weak but he is strong.
Yes, Jesus loves me.
Yes, Jesus loves me.
Yes, Jesus loves me.
The Bible tells me so.
I look forward to seeing my family again.
I look forward to seeing my friends again.
I look forward to seeing Jesus face-to-face.
I look forward to hugging everyone again.
So whether *you* or *I*
Cross the finish line *first*,
Let's prepare our hearts,
Walk the walk, walk in peace and in love,
Be bright lights,
Shine for Jesus,
And be clamorously foolish.
Let's be positive we will make it.
We just don't know *who'll* cross the finish line first,
So let's be ready, be instant in season,

Press in to God's heart as we press on courageously
Till God calls us home to be with Him forever...*forever*!
Forever...is a long, long, long, long, long, long, long, time!
Glory to God! ☺

5.19.03
John 3:16: "For God so loved the world, that he gave his only begotten Son, that whosoever believeth in him should not perish, but have everlasting life."

40

Pain...a Friend?

~

Pain, I've been told,
Can be your friend.
If you burn your hand,
Pain tells you to move it or lose it.
In my case, at this time,
Pain tells me
The medicine is...doing its job!
Lab work showed my white cell count was 1.5.
It needed to be higher.
The nurse gave me a needle
In my tummy...four days in a row.
Yes—in my tummy.
The medicine results in adolescent cells
Being pulled down to produce more blood
Because there are no more mature cells.
In just days, the count will be up.
This means my chemo treatment in six days
Need not be canceled.
That is good, because I look forward to moving soon—
Before the end of August.
I will be in Canada before my birthday.
So when it comes to pain,

I understand why this is happening.
In the natural, the realm of the five senses,
It fits perfectly as a piece to a puzzle,
But…it is not yet complete
Because my life consists of the spiritual man, too.
Consequently, I've learned some things
About my inheritance as a child of God.
Jesus paid the price for me to be healed.
Jesus paid the price for me to be pain-free.

Jesus paid the price for me to be saved, healed,
and delivered.
I'm determined to make sure His blood was not shed
in vain.

How do I achieve such a thing?
Receive it all: salvation, healing, and deliverance.
I submit to God first,
Take authority over the enemy, the devil.
Put him and his fruit, such as sickness and pain,
Under my feet where they belong.
I do what God taught me to do:
Speak the things that are not
As though they are.
I make sure my spirit man controls my body,
Not vice versa.
I speak to my body.
I tell it to line up with the Word of God.
I command pain to cease.
I command every organ, tissue, and cell
To function the way God created it to function,

And I forbid any malfunction.
I am healed by the stripes laid on Jesus Christ (1 Peter 2:24).
I am not going to be healed,
Because I am already healed, and I receive it by faith.
I'm not moved by circumstances;
Circumstances are subject to change.
I speak God's Word.
I work the Word, and it works.
There's nothing spooky about it at all.
The Word of God is full of life.
I speak words of life.
The more I do so,

The sooner the manifestation
Of what I am speaking of.
God's Word will not come back void (Isaiah 55:11);
It will accomplish what it is sent to do.
Greater is He that is in me than he that is in the world
(1 John 4:4).

It is because of Christ in me,
The hope of glory,
That I have confidence and faith to receive.
I receive daily as the Holy Spirit fills me
From head to toe.
It is an ongoing process.
Like the song says…
He's changing me.
I've been made in the image of God.
I am fearfully and wonderfully made.
No weapon formed against me shall prosper (Isaiah 51:17).

Every tongue that rises up against me
Shall be condemned—
This is the heritage of the children of God.
The Lord is my Shepherd (Psalms 23:1);
I shall not want.
Therefore, I have no lack.
God is prospering me in every area of my life.
There are no limits with God.
I delight myself in Him (Psalms 37:4).
He gives me the desires of my heart.
I am fearfully and wonderfully made (Isaiah 44:2).
It is no secret what God can do.
God is no respecter of persons.
He has no favorites.
He loves everyone equally and unconditionally.
The tree is known by its fruit.
Out of the abundance of the heart (Matthew 12:34),
The mouth speaks.

So, when it comes to pain,
It has to go
In Jesus's name.

5.29.03
Hebrews 4:12: "For the word of God is quick and powerful, and sharper than any twoedged sword, piercing even to the dividing asunder of soul and spirit, and of the joints and marrow, and is a discerner of the thoughts and intents of the heart."

41

Do I Have to Write It?

Kids are so unprejudiced,
So completely accepting of change.
Adults stop in their tracks
When they see something different,
Such as a woman wearing a turban or a wig.
Then they stare and stare.
One can almost hear the wheels turning
As their minds ask questions:
Is it a wig or isn't it?
Does she have cancer or not?

Then they check from head to toe
As if clothing could tell.
When they realize I am making eye contact,
They look down or away quickly,
Yet I was about to smile and say, "Hi."
It doesn't stop there.
I went to the sanctuary and sat down.

A particular man kept staring.
I wondered why he was so intrigued.
I'd been to many services—

He hadn't even shaken hands before.
So what do I do?
Maintain my focus on Jesus
And say a little prayer for the man.
If seeing change is all it takes
To stop him in his tracks,
I pray he never has to endure changes caused by cancer.
Bless him, Lord, with some compassion, please.
Lord, thanks that *You* walk with me every step
And You do not stare.
You look at me lovingly...always.
I love You, Lord; You are so good to me.
Thanks for squeezing my hand a bit tighter.
It helps.

6.2.03
Psalms 34:19: "Many are the afflictions of the righteous: but the Lord delivereth him out of them all."

42

I Don't Want To

I don't want to be sick.
I don't want to feel weak and listless.
I don't want my joints to ache.
I don't want to stay out of the sun.
I don't want to spend hours on end in bed.
I don't want to draw attention because I'm wearing a wig.
I didn't ask for cancer, and I don't want it
Or any of the side effects.
So now what?
I've prayed for healing,
Claimed my healing in Jesus's name,
Claimed the promises in Isaiah 53, 1 Peter 2:24,
Matthew 18:19, and Jeremiah 32:27.
I speak words of life: the Word of God.
I submit to God.
I resist the devil, and he flees.
Days pass by—even months—since the diagnosis.
My faith is in God, not man.
Yet I submit to the doctors and take medical treatment…
I expect my body to line up
With the Word of God.
This means when the scan is taken
Just after the sixth chemo treatment,

It will show my body is 100 percent free of any tumors.
This will bring glory to God,
And I believe the report of the Lord (1 Peter 2:24).
God has heard and answered my prayers.
God has heard and answered the prayers of many
others, too.
God told me right from the beginning
That it would not be easy
But that He would stand beside me every step of the way,

And He would see me through!
I believe God is doing exactly that, so I'll praise Him
Before the circumstances line up with the Word,
When the circumstances line up with the Word,
And after the circumstances line up with the Word,
Because *that* is *faith*!
And I can't please God without it.
I aim to please God!
There is nothing more important to do.
Man is limited in helping me.
God is not limited.
It is that simple.
Even my doctor agrees.
Praise the Lord!
Besides, having a pity party never helped anyone.
No one would come but me anyway.
Praise the Lord!

6.21.03
Hebrews 11:1: "Now faith is the substance of things hoped for, the evidence of things not seen."

43

Cabin Fever

~~~

As I HAVE spent time in prayer for three hours, the Lord has really impressed on me the importance of light from the sun and from the Son as well. After being diagnosed with lung cancer, I've been told that I'm not to be in the direct sunlight. Many times, I have heard women complain when they've had three days of rain, and they are inside the house with the kids. They really want the light. They are craving light and sunshine and brightness. So what do I do?

I submit to God and resist the devil; he flees. I stand on the Word of God. I am healed; I have already been healed, and the manifestation of that has to line up with the Word no matter what the circumstances look like or what the doctor's report says. The Word works, so I continue to speak the Word. That's what Jesus did. It is as simple as that. As for the doctor's report and directions...I submit to what the doctor says to do, and I do stay out of the direct sunlight.

This is somewhat like those who have been given a prescription to wear eye glasses: they go for prayer, receive prayer, believe they receive their healing, stand on the Word, break their glasses and throw them away, and then they find out they need them to drive the car. They really do, because they do not see the stop signs. It just proves that God will cause the doctor's report to line up with the Word of God as the patient continues to speak the Word of God because that is what Jesus did, and you cannot add light. I begin where the root of the problem is: deep within. I begin by adding light—by adding the Word of God, which is pure light—pure, unadulterated light and truth filling my life from within as I study, meditate, and speak the Word; that light shines through to the outside for others to see, bringing glory to God.

Complacency kills: those are two words that the Holy Spirit nudged me about this morning. I believe it is because the onus is on me as a Christian to feed myself the Word of God, not to wait for the pastor to feed me a couple of times a week. It is up to me to see that I am fed daily, the same as it is in the natural, and I don't go without very many meals (except when on a fast). Consequently, I need to buckle down and get more of the Word in me, and then before long, I will be able to sit out in the sun just like everyone else, as well as have the Son in me, shining through for all to see. That brings glory to God, and that is what it is all about. He is changing me from the inside; that is the victory that Jesus paid the price for me to have. So, what do I do?

I'll write a book telling others how I came through with the help of the Lord, so that those who are going through valleys can experience the same victory that I have experienced. Notice I said *have*, not *had*. They can experience the same victory that I have because the Word of God says that God is no respecter of persons. He loves obedience—habitual, not spasmodic, obedience.

I pray these words are encouraging and inspiring to you, my readers, and that you will continue to read as I continue to share that which God has shown me as He brings me through this valley, this very deep valley of the shadow of death I walk through—and it is the Holy Spirit that is standing beside me every step of the way, just as He said He would. He also said that it would not be easy but that He would see me through. That's all I needed to know.

I've got it like a fire, a flame inside my gut (if you will), burning eternally with life and hope and encouragement, no matter how dark it may look on the other side. I am on my way out of darkness and carnality in Jesus's name. Hallelujah. Glory to God!

After attending church this morning, I realized there are some situations that will arise that I need to know how to deal with effectively. One is when someone says, "You're *healed...* in Jesus's name." I agree—in Jesus's name. My body is telling me something different when the red cell count and the white cell counts are lower than normal, yet I am healed in Jesus's name. The person that says, "You're *healed* in Jesus's name!" means well and means to encourage me. I realize this, and for this I am grateful.

On the other hand, I am learning it is only those that have been touched by cancer—whether they have been diagnosed or are a family member or a friend of someone who has been diagnosed with cancer—who have the compassion that is really needed when they feel led to minister to someone who has been diagnosed with cancer.

The reason is that they understand that even though the person is standing on the Word and believing in the manifestation of healing (and is not in denial of the cancer diagnosis but is denying its right to stay in that body), he or she still needs a hug and still needs someone who will weep with him or her, as well as laugh with him or her, once in a while.

Being dogmatic somehow doesn't cut through to the point of comforting my spirit one bit, yet being compassionate does. God's ways are higher. Jesus is our example. There were times when He wept also; it was not a sin. Both men and women have tear ducts for a reason. It is not a sin for a cancer victim to weep while believing simultaneously in that healing as he or she speaks the Word of God daily and awaits the manifestation of the healing in Jesus's name.

Hugs are a big part of the healing process, I am convinced. Hugs are huge doses of medicine that taste good every time! Have you had your hug today? If no one is there with you, that's okay; just remember Jesus is the best hugger anyway, so ask Him for a healing hug as to Him you draw nigh. He hugs me "from the inside."

6.9.03
Jeremiah 31:3: "The Lord hath appeared of old unto me, saying, Yea, I have loved thee with an everlasting love: therefore with lovingkindness I have drawn thee."

44

You've Gotta Do What You've Gotta Do!

∼⌁

THIS IS THE first time I've taken notes this way, but sometimes you've gotta do what you've gotta do! (I recorded this because I was too weak to keep up with my writing and typing.) This is June 27, 2003, Friday afternoon. I thought I was going to go to church tonight to the prayer meeting, but I've been in bed all day and barely had the strength to get up and go to the bathroom. As far as feelings go, my body is just so weak it is an effort to even sit up and drink coffee, so what do I do?

I have books here that I am trying to read to make good use of my time. One of the books has a chapter on time management and the importance of it. It is a little difficult, to say the least, not to get frustrated when time is slipping by—not just the pages for each day but the months since my lung surgery in March; now we are almost into July, and it seems like my life is wasting by, yet life has never been more important to me. So, what do you do? Having a pity party doesn't help.

You talk to Jesus, and you listen to Him. You ask the Holy Spirit to help you. You're thankful that you have a best friend who never leaves you or forsakes you—a best friend who knows how to comfort you in the good times and in the bad…a best friend who will have a *rhema* word for you. This one is for me; ask for yours. He is my friend and honors His words to me. He said, **"It will not be easy, but I will see you through...I will stand beside you every step of the way."** Well, these steps seem to be going kind of slowly right now, but that is okay because like the Lord said, He'll see me through.

By faith my strength is returning. I am healed in the name of Jesus by the stripes laid on Jesus Christ. God's Word will not come back void; it will accomplish what it is sent to do. I submit to God. I resist the devil; he flees. I rebuke discouragement, anxiety, stress, sorrow, and grief in Jesus's name. I throw myself into Your arms, Jesus, and I thank You that You know how to comfort me. I thank You that I am not falling. I thank You that I am walking onward and upward out of this valley and on to the next mountaintop experience with You, and I will give You the glory (sigh). Nothing is too hard for You. You are the Lord, the God of all flesh (Jeremiah 32:27).

Right now, it seems every person's face that comes to mind whom I could just talk to for a little bit of encouragement is someone who is not home in the daytime, but I don't think that is a coincidence. God wants me leaning on Him: it's that simple. He's the only one who never lets me down, so I might as well go to Him in the first place and not run to people. (I sing a cappella, "My God is an awesome God. He reigns in heaven and earth with wisdom, power, and love. My God is an awesome God.")

Father, I thank You for the peace deep in my heart even though there are tears. Even though there are questions, it does not matter. It is okay. That's okay. This too shall pass. I'll just enjoy looking at the fresh flowers that are by the TV—the bright colors; I'll enjoy the ceiling fan; I'll enjoy the central air; I'll enjoy having access to all these Bibles and good books, plus the benefit of prayers from many people. I ask You to bless them for praying for me, Lord. Bless them, bless them, bless them, and let them know I appreciate their prayers.

I love You, Jesus. Thank You for helping me, for encouraging me. I love You, Lord. xoxo

6.27.03
Psalms 4:4–5: "Stand in awe, and sin not: commune with your own heart upon your bed, and be still. Selah. Offer the sacrifices of righteousness, and put your trust in the Lord."

45

Hello, Walls

~

HELLO, WALLS. THE walls I'm looking at are in a hospital. I was admitted last night, Wednesday, July 9, 2003, four months after lung surgery, with a temperature of 101 degrees Fahrenheit, vomiting, a sore throat, a headache, and a staph infection. It was 12:30 a.m. before the paperwork was done and everyone left my room so I could go to sleep.

I cried because I felt like it was a defeat. I'd done so well for so long, and I believed that brought glory to God—the fact that I was able to continue going to church—and now here I was, laid up. It wasn't that it was my fault or had been caused by anything I did, yet I felt like it was a defeat.

The nurses were very good with me, especially one nurse. She said, "It's a setback, but that's all it is." After I got to sleep and woke up in the morning, I began to appreciate the quietness in the room.

When I looked out the window this morning and saw small, white clouds—many of them—it looked like God had just hand-painted those clouds in the sky for me. It made me smile, and then a bird flew up by my window, made a little circle, and left. Again, it was like God was saying, **"Good morning."**

Then one airplane passed. It was a reminder that I'd be flying to Canada soon so to keep my chin up. It's really very simple to recognize God on a daily basis, and it's wonderful.

FYI: I recorded this on a little tape recorder because I was too sick to write, yet when the words are burning within, they must come forth. God put that passion within me as Jesus kept revealing Himself to me time and again.

7.9.03
Deuteronomy 6:5: "And thou shalt love the Lord thy God with all thine heart, and with all thy soul, and with all thy might."

46

Step by Step

~

While I sit on a chair,
Looking at my hospital bed,
Many thoughts are racing
In my head.
I know I'm where I need to be
Because of the way my body is responding (to chemo).
Yet it is currently quite difficult
To get my heart to sing.
I know the Lord is by my side,
Fully aware of everything that's going on,
Yet when it comes to feeling spiritual,
That feeling has somehow...gone.
I talk to the Lord, and He talks to me.
I read my Bible and listen to sermons on TV.
My prayers aren't as fervent or as zealous,
Yet I'm confident He hears me.
I speak to my body, too—
Tell it to line up with the Word.
I stand on the promises of God,
Knowing my body has heard.
When weakness tries to take charge,
I say, "The joy of the Lord is my strength," night and day.

When a tendency for self-pity arises,
I simply resist it and say, "No way!"
Before I know it, days have passed by.
My body has something different to say.
It is lining up with the Word of God,
And the doctor says, "You can go home today."
It was just a slight affliction.
This too shall pass, and it did once again.
I'm pressing in to God's heart, and on.
Chin up, shoulders back, and no pain.
Glory to God again and again!

9.5.03

Ephesians 6:10–13: Finally, my brethren, be strong in the Lord, and in the power of his might. Put on the whole armour of God, that ye may be able to stand against the wiles of the devil. For we wrestle not against flesh and blood, but against principalities, against powers, against the rulers of the darkness of this world, against spiritual wickedness in high places. Wherefore take unto you the whole armour of God, that ye may be able to withstand in the evil day, and having done all, to stand.

47

Compromise Kills

~

When Christians lower their standards
By allowing sin in their homes,
They will have blood on their hands
Unless the sin is exposed and stopped.
Sin is serious.
The wages of sin are death.
When a Christian refuses to raise a standard,
That is putting someone else before God.
God is a jealous God.
He hates sin.
Christians need to hate sin, too.
When the truth is spoken in love
And darkness is exposed,
The sinner has a decision to make:
Repent and turn from the wicked way
Or continue in sin unashamedly...
As a loving God woos...
And satan lures...
God's ways really do satisfy.
The flesh dies hard.
No one can serve two masters.
It is a spiritual battle.

God will not force anyone to do anything.
He gave everyone a free will.
He challenges everyone to climb up higher spiritually.
Compromise costs much.
It is not God's way.
God wants all or nothing.
In Revelation 3:16, He said, **"If you are lukewarm
I'll spew you out of my mouth."**
There's no misunderstanding such clear words.

God wants His children to be hot,
Not lukewarm or cold.
He gave His best when He sent His Son.
He asks the best of each of His children, too.
If you love God, you'll obey God.
You'll hate sin and be grieved
By the things that grieve God.
When your friend gets hurt, you hurt.
When you compromise, you hurt God
As well as yourself.
I don't ever want to hurt God.
My prayer is that backsliders
Will be convicted by the Holy Spirit
As He lovingly woos them closer
To the heart of God.
Heaven is real, as is hell.
Compromise leads to more sin,
Like quicksand burying someone inch by inch.
The choice is yours…Jesus is calling you.
Raise up a standard for righteousness' sake.

7.14.03

Revelation 3:16-18: "So then because thou art lukewarm, and neither cold nor hot, I will spew thee out of my mouth. Because thou sayest, I am rich, and increased with goods, and have need of nothing; and knowest not that thou art wretched, and miserable, and poor, and blind, and naked: I counsel thee to buy of me gold tried in the fire, that thou mayest be rich; and white raiment, that thou mayest be clothed, and that the shame of thy nakedness do not appear; and anoint thine eyes with eyesalve, that thou mayest see."

48

A Coping Tool

~~

Who would have thought
A woman ill from a staph infection
With fever and vomiting
Could still…in her heart…simultaneously
Be praying to God sincerely
And yes, even praising Him…
A relationship with Jesus Christ
Is the reason why
It can be done.
Not religion— relationship,
But that's not all. I know, because "she" was me.
As I lay with a gold chain and gold locket
Around my neck, gently moving with me,
My thoughts transferred from the exterior
To the photos inside the locket:
A photo of each of my parents smiling.
I knew they were both in heaven,
Yet the thought of those photos
Somehow brought comfort
And helped close any gap between heaven and earth.
God can use anything for a point of contact
To release what is needed,

And I needed comfort.
My pretty gold locket with pink roses
Became for me a coping tool.
My eyes were still on Jesus,
Yet He allowed me this pleasure.
He knew my family was sixteen hundred miles away
As I lay in that hospital bed.
No matter how severe the storm, it's okay
Because God's peace deep within is my umpire.
He knows how to get His love to me from head to toe,
Whether by a word, a vision, a picture, a locket, or peace...I
know! ☺

7.15.03
**Nahum 1:7: "The Lord is good, a strong hold in the day
of trouble; and he knoweth them that trust in Him."**

49

Radiation Room Routines

~⁓

THE RADIATION TREATMENTS proved to be humiliating because the radiation was targeted over my upper lung, which meant my breasts were bare some of the time, and there were several men and women in attendance prior to the actual treatment. The first day was the most difficult because of the unknown. There was no pain in receiving the radiation, but there was stress to deal with again.

Firstly, the so-called bed I lay on was raised very high in the air, and it was very narrow. This made me wonder how some people who were quite overweight managed to stay on; it was challenging not to shiver simply because of how cold it was, let alone from nerves.

I had to raise my arms over my head and rest them into a fabric that formed a custom pillow. Each time I went in, the mold was placed in position for me. I have a few tattoos now because of how I was marked prior to receiving radiation. (Not real tattoos—I was marked with indelible ink though. ☺) It is important to pinpoint the exact area, and this is how the doctors mark it so there are no mistakes.

I think I had a total of twenty-eight radiation treatments. The radiation resulted in blisters forming on my back and shoulder area. The ointment did not help. It did not happen until near the end of the treatments, but postponing treatment until my back healed was not an option. I had to tough it out even though it was sore, itchy, and felt like needles pricking me if I scratched it. The third ointment prescribed brought some relief, thankfully. Knowing I only had a few more treatments made it more tolerable.

The doctor told me my throat would probably get very sore and feel like a cracker was stuck in it when I swallowed. He kept asking me how I was feeling. I went five days a week once the treatments started. I was fine. He could not understand why I was okay. He kept asking me, and it was almost funny because he was so puzzled. Finally, I said, "There are a lot of people praying for me." He said, "There's nothing wrong with that."

Then I told him *what* I prayed. I said it was a bit nerve racking just prior to getting the radiation after everyone but me had left the room, so I prayed while I waited. I said, "God, I ask you to send Your angels to surround me and flap their wings or do whatever they have to do to stop me from having any adverse side effects from this radiation, in Jesus's name." I said that prayer every single time I had radiation treatments, and my side effects were nil except for the blisters near the end. My head did not try to figure it out.

I just prayed what the Holy Spirit led me to pray, and it worked. It is good not to limit God or put Him in a box. When it is the eleventh hour, the prayers are short, to the point, and power-packed with faith. My confidence was in the Lord. He said He'd bring me through! Besides, the cross

Jesus hung on was not padded, and I surely have never sweat drops of blood.

I was learning God heals in different ways, such as miracles and instant healings; but some are healed through the use of medicine, chemotherapy, radiation, doctors, nurses, and so on. I also learned mankind is limited. God is not. The Creator of the entire universe, and of my body, surely is capable of healing without restrictions. God is a big God. Like my motto states: small world, big God! ☺

Folks, this is a little insert as I update something that happened in that room that should not have happened. It wounded me so deeply I could not share it until now. When I was in position to receive the radiation treatment, medical men, staff, stood around my bed, as I lay there naked from the waist up. A woman entered, a nurse. She stood by my left side, said nothing as she gently reach out and pulled the sheet up to cover my breasts totally. Noone said a word.

Her actions told me this is the way I should have been covered for all 28 treatments. Who knew? This nurse knew. Immediately, shame flooded me and hot tears streamed into my ears as I lay there helpless thinking of all the previous exposures. I could not stop weeping. Don't tell me little things don't mean a lot. One nurse with compassion and not afraid to reach with help.

If you were a man lying there instead of me, how would you feel if your... shall I say 'private parts' were exposed to the nurses, as you lay helpless, instructed not to move? They surround your bed staring at your unexcited anatomy. I daresay any 'Macho Man' within departs as you wait for them to leave so the radiation could begin? Everyone hurts somewhere.

Everyone. The flesh dies hard. Let's aim to crucify the flesh. Healing runs in God's family. He does not change.

Genesis 1:1:
"In the beginning God created the heaven and the earth."

50

The Pampered Patient

~~~

Last week I was a chemo patient
At Northwest Texas Hospital.
During the four days and four nights in Amarillo,
Every single person who entered my room
Showed kindness, promptness, and compassion;
Was smiling with each meal brought in;
Spoke softly at 4:00 a.m.; then...took my blood pressure.
They knew when to leave and when to linger a bit.
I enjoyed our spontaneous conversations immensely.
Many people continued to check if I needed something,
Not just once or twice a day but very often.
I saw compassion in their eyes.
I appreciated the excellent care.
In fact, I remember thinking to myself
That if I just...wasn't...sick...
This would be like a hotel room
And I'd be the pampered "patient."
The food was hot, tasty, and plentiful,
Whether my appetite was up to par or not.
I never heard any strife among staff.
In fact, there were times I heard laughter
And cheerful voices...it warmed my heart.

When it comes to needles, I cringe somewhat,
But for the most part I had minimal pain.
Forgive me, but I wondered if there was currently
A quality control inspection being done.
Yet the excellent care continued
Day and night...they were so sincere.
I'm home now, but I gained a lot!
I brought memories with me
Of smiling eyes and faces,
Compassion, love, concern—
A team...of the best...working in unity...
Helping others and helping me.
Thank you, everyone!
And God abundantly bless thee!

Lovingly,
Linda Lou Jones,
The Pampered Patient.

P.S. One thing I did pray specifically for
Was a new mattress
Because someone slept in this one before
Without a doubt...
(The whole city I think!) ☺

**P.P.S. I pray y'all do your job as unto the Lord
Because if it would have been Jesus in that bed...
He would have received A+ care!
"Your labor is not in vain."
You are loved and appreciated.**

FYI: A nurse told me when this poem was posted on a bulletin board in the hospital, staff from the floor with cancer patients only, as well as staff from other floors came to read it during their coffee breaks.

Y'all made me smile.
☺
Thank you.

51

Big-Screen View

~~

As I sat in a recliner receiving a chemotherapy treatment,
My spirit soared; the joy of the Lord poured forth, too.
People were interceding for me—
People who knew how to pray through.
Describing the incredible rush,
For lack of a better word,
Is not easy to do.
I find it humbling
To be dependent on the prayers of others.
Yet I praise God for the obedience of the intercessors.
I just wish more people knew
The incredible good that is done
And that more intercessors knew, too.
God is answering all those prayers.
I give Him praise and glory
And thank you, too…so very much.
Maybe someday God will show a "big-screen view"
Of what happens in the spirit realm
When intercessors pray and pray through.
It would be an action-packed video;
That I do know, and I don't mean maybe.

Just knowing people are praying for me
Is being on the receiving end
Of something money can't buy.
There *are* things money can't buy.
Money is not the motivator for intercessors.
The Holy Spirit gives people the unction to pray.
Using one's heavenly language (Ephesians 6:17–18) assures
The perfect will of God is being prayed.
It's a win-win situation.

I must say
I really, really like
God's way!

7.16.03
Romans 8:26–27: "Likewise the Spirit also helpeth our infirmities: for we know not what we should pray for as we ought: but the Spirit itself maketh intercession for us with groanings which cannot be uttered. And he that searcheth the hearts knoweth what is the mind of the Spirit, because he maketh intercession for the saints according to the will of God."

FYI: Having a chemotherapy treatment simply means I sat in a recliner chair with all the tubes running from a plastic bag of chemicals into my body intravenously. It did not hurt. I could visit with other chemo patients. Sometimes there were several in the same room. We could watch TV, too. I chose to write my poems to get my mind off the stress. The first treatment took eleven hours to administer. The following treatments were several hours each. As I knew the treatment could cause complications, even a stroke, I did ask for prayer specifically during the times of the treatment. Fear has to be put under the patient's feet. It is called "taking dominion" in Jesus's name, and it worked for me…totally!

Update:
7.26.03, 3:00 a.m.: Eight days after first chemo treatment, I feel good.

FYI: I was not sick from the treatment. The more diffi-cult part was keeping track of all the pills I had to take at spe-cific times. It was necessary to set the alarm every hour the first night after treatment to take my pills, which helped me not be sick. My eyes wouldn't close anyway because I felt so wired the first night after treatment. That changed as adjust-ments were made to the chemicals I received.

The day after my first chemo treatment, a new chemo friend called and insisted I go with her to the high-school event for cancer. I actually walked all the way around the track holding a huge banner along with several other can-cer survivors in the front of the pack. It was an honor and a thrill.

Also, it was a shock to see my oncology doctor and his wife cheering me on from the sidelines! A lot of people were there, and it proved to be a time of making new memo-ries under the bright Texas sunshine. I wore a purple T-shirt given to survivors, and we made a paper-chain link. Each person's chain represented the number of years they had been cancer-free. It was inspiring for me to meet someone who had been cancer-free seventeen years. I braved the elements wearing my black turban and broke through the barriers of

pride and self-consciousness. It was yet another new beginning, ending with the lighting of candles symbolic of those in
attendance as well as others who had since passed.

There was a live band playing great music. My toes were
tapping as I sat and listened, even though the valley was very
deep. Who would have thought I could rise up from that bed
that had held me down for months since surgery and make
it around the track? **Thank God my motivator, San Clay,
extended the invitation.** She gave me her sunglasses on that
eventful day, plus much inspiration, courage, and love—a true
example of having "been there, done that." Now, in turn, she
was reaching out to help others face their mountains. Sounds
like something Jesus would do.

**Matthew 7:12: "Therefore all things whatsoever ye would
that men should do to you, do ye even so to them: for this
is the law and the prophets."**

52

A Tight Squeeze

~~

My hand is squeezing Jesus's hand so tightly,
I hope I don't hurt Him,
Because I don't ever want to hurt Him.
I don't ever want to hurt anyone.
He hasn't complained that I'm pinching.
In fact, I think I see a grin on His face:
An inner delight bursting through
Because He likes it
When I draw closer.
He likes it when I lean on Him.
He likes it when I trust Him
And walk by faith.
He likes being close to me,
And I like being close to Him.
He makes me feel safe, sheltered,
Calm in the midst of a storm—
Like a woman should feel
When she's with her best friend.
His hand is so strong and warm,

Clutching my hand purposefully.
Jesus knows I need Him so much.
I know I can do nothing without Him.
He is always in position.
My position is to be next to Him,
Close to His heart,
With my heart open at all times—
Daring to be vulnerable,
Willing to yield completely,
Staying close so He can whisper
His secrets to me.
And He does.
Praise the Lord!

Side Note: In my efforts to climb up higher spiritually and deepen my relationship with Jesus as my spiritual husband, holding His hand was an image that helped incredibly, although it was not meant to bring Him to my level. I for sure was looking up.

7.23.03
Jeremiah 33:3: "Call to me and I will answer thee, and show thee great and mighty things, which thou knowest not."

53

Free and Happy

~⌒

Something happened to me.
I knew it tonight.
Yet I'm not sure what.
Yet, I *do* know...
I've been set free!
The grief is gone.
It left completely.
I went to a prayer meeting.
Later, at home, I picked up my microphone,
Started singing from my heart.
In the car I sang some more.
Something was happening to me,
And I knew it.
I'd been touched from the *inside*.
Jesus touched me.
I'd been set free.
All the heartache was gone.
I shared with a friend.
Then I saw double doors opening—
Exterior doors opening outward,
Welcoming me.
I was reminded of the doors

At the top of a long set of stairs at Grace Cathedral.
Grace is the church where I was saved and matured quickly.
The open doors are symbolic of two things:
A new beginning
And double…
Double everything!
God is in the restoration business.
Praise His holy name.
I believe things are going to start happening
Fast…because it is time…
For the manifestation of some miracles I've seen in the
spirit.
I'm not only *free*,
I'm *happy*! ☺

**Joel 2:25: "And I will restore to you the years that the
locust hath eaten, the cankerworm, and the caterpillar,
and the palmerworm, my great army which I sent among
you."**

54

Transplant Preparations

~⁀

It does not seem coincidental
That three different plants I see need to be transplanted,
Kind of like me.
A larger pot is needed for the plants to thrive.
They've outgrown their current home.
It's time to uproot so they'll survive.
Transition is not easy, but it is most necessary,
Whether it be for a plant or for me.
Although new topsoil is used
As well as much water and loving care,
There is usually a bit of a setback
As the roots have been bare.
Yet with much love and daily pampering,
Roots have a way of being soothed,
Even desiring to once again sing.

The plant looks okay because everything is in place,
But it takes time before restoration takes place.
Bit by bit, restoration will occur as each day passes by.
A new environment, a new home, family, and friends
Are like water to the roots as each day ends,
Soothing frayed nerves, calming each fear.

Soon the plant relaxes and settles in more comfortably.
Simultaneously, the Lord wipes away each tear.
Hurts and wounds are released and healed.
God's love pours forth hour by hour,
So I'll not dread the change;
Rather, I'm to welcome it readily,
Knowing it is what is best for me.
I'll choose to look beyond the apparent setback
That occurs at the time of transplanting,
Knowing the best is yet to come.
In fact, I'll be producing many blossoms.

My leaves will not be wilted at all.
I'll be a fruit-bearing tree for the kingdom of God
Because I was obedient and answered His call.
He beckoned me to "come to Canada."
He called me, so here I am, Lord.
Use me—I yield willingly.
I don't want to be where you don't want me.
I'm in the center of Your perfect will.
Thank You for leading me step by step each day.
I can do nothing without You, Lord.
I'm Yours; use me if You can.
In Jesus's name, I pray.

John 15:5: "I am the vine, ye are the branches: He that abideth in me, and I in him, the same bringeth forth much fruit: for without me ye can do nothing."

55

The Final Release

~9

How can I help abused women?
Donate the books that helped me.
God will speak to their hearts
And set them free.
I can move on to Canada,
Yet leave the books behind.
Jesus will minister to each one.
I really don't mind.
I'm told they can be helped this way.
Painful as it is to let go—
My books are kind of like my babies,
Don't you know?
I can't take them with me,
But I can trust God to be there.
He'll help me move on
Somewhere.
If the women will read and read,
There is much they will learn each day.
I did, and I'm so glad.
Also, I did pray.
Now I'm a survivor of abuse:
Mental, physical, and emotional.

I'm a survivor of cancer,
A mental breakdown decades ago,
Rejection and abandonment, attempted murder,
Poverty, manipulation, control,
Witchcraft, Russian roulette, children kidnapped,
Fear, betrayal, divorce, and yet more.
I'm a survivor of every mountain I faced,
And I faced them all
Because God led me through every valley.
Now, according to Romans 8:28,

God will turn this all around.
The valley inverted is a very high mountaintop—
Not one, but many.
Consequently, I will now be
Like the cream of the crop
That rises to the top
Not once, but many times!
Like a clock that will not stop,
I'll just keep ticking and ticking
Like a syncopated clock.
My hand is in the hand of the Lord
As He leads me from glory to glory.
All I do is sing, speak, write, pray,
Be His witness every day.
Let my light shine,
Be clamorously foolish as I share
What Jesus has done for me,
How Jesus revealed himself to me:
How He helped me,
How He set me free

To be a fully yielded vessel,
Yet poured out and full
Simultaneously.
It is no longer I who live
But Christ who lives in me.
To God be the glory.
Bottom line:
I truly am not going back home to die
But to live.
Christ lives in me.
To God be the glory!

7.26.03
Proverbs 18:16: "A man's gift maketh room for him, and bringeth him before great men."

56

Harvesting Thoughts

~)

The trees are loaded with leaves.
One tree is heavily laden with green apples.
On the wire high above the fence
Is one red-breasted bird, sitting patiently.
It may look to the bird's eyes
Like nothing is happening this morning,
But the truth is…
There's a whole lot going on.
Aside from the cat chasing a dog
In one backyard,
Aside from the dogs barking
From their side of the fence
When they hear the commotion,
Aside from the sound
Of a neighbor's car door closing,
Aside from the leaves waving
As a gentle breeze emerges…
Yes, there's a whole lot going on.
The goings-on I just mentioned
Reflect what one sees with the natural eye.
Mankind is a spirit, lives in a body,
And has a soul consisting of mind, will, emotions.

There is a whole lot more going on
Than what one sees with the natural eye.
It is a spiritual battle.
Whether you believe it or not
Does not change the truth.
With spiritually opened eyes
Because of the scriptures I prayed
In Jesus's name, I see
Angels lining the perimeter of the home and property;
The blood of Jesus has been applied, covering everything.
The Spirit of the Lord is upon me
Morning, noon, and night.
He has put His words in my mouth
And given me boldness to speak those words of truth.
My focus is on Jesus.
He reveals much to me
Prophetically:
Sometimes through prophecy given at church,
Sometimes through prophecy given by a neighbor,
Sometimes through a song or a sermon,
Sometimes through the Word of God.
There's no limit to how it can be done.
Once the prophecy is received,
I check deep within to see if I have a witness,
An inner green light—or is it red?
God has ways of confirming to me
A Word He has given prophetically.
I wait with spiritually opened ears and heart
Expecting, anticipating, like a pregnant woman
When God has confirmed the Word given.
Then there is a waiting period.

A time of gestation…if you will.
My faith has a chance to grow,
As does my patience,
Because I am called to walk by faith,
Not by sight…"can't please God without faith."
So what do I do in the interim?
From the time the seed took root
Until the day of manifestation,
Do I let my feelings rule, or do I walk by faith?
The decision is mine.
The more I am in the Word,
The less I will waver.
"A double-minded man is unstable in all his ways."
Daily, it is a spiritual battle.
The devil wants to steal the seed that was planted.
The mind is the battleground.
Thoughts come to my mind—negative thoughts,
Tormenting thoughts, discouraging thoughts:
Words that paint negative pictures.
Do I allow the words to keep coming
Until they are like a nest that's been built,
A stronghold…?
Or do I recognize the fruit of the devil,
The father of lies,
And use the authority I've been given
As a child of God?
Sometimes I use the sword (God's Word) immediately.
Sometimes, if my carnal nature is surfacing,
I listen and contemplate,
Allow my feelings to toss and turn
While meditating on the negative thoughts

Until my spirit is absolutely vexed.
Then I'm a mess.
It takes more effort and more time
To untangle a tangled web
Than it does to nip it in the bud.
Consequently, it is up to me
Whether I stay free.
It is not anyone else walking in my shoes.
I know what is going on in my head.
I know how to take authority in Jesus's name
Over thoughts that come that are not of God...
When I rebuke those thoughts immediately
Then focus on Jesus and His sweet presence,
It is well with my soul.
When I stay in the Word, I'm positive, too, and encouraged.
When I offer a sacrifice of praise to God,
Soon it is not a sacrifice.
I *want* to!
So don't be taken in by what you see.
There's a reason you're right where you are.
Bloom where you are planted.
You're going far.
It may not look like it today,
But that's okay.
This is our season
For some R&R (rest and relaxation).
The best is yet to come.
God will not let you down.
Look beyond the circumstances,
Walk by faith, live by faith.
You'll not go wrong.

Hold on to Jesus.
Ride out your storm.
He will never leave you.
The next season is…
Harvest time! ☺

7.27.03
Genesis 8:22: "While the earth remaineth, seedtime and harvest, and cold and heat, and summer and winter, and day and night shall not cease."

57

A Deeper Walk

~~

I've been sitting up in bed,
Wondering why it hurts so much today
To do such a simple thing
As giving my books away.
Several hundred books—but they are still
Just books, large and small.
So I asked the Holy Spirit to help me understand,
Because in giving, I am answering His call.
The Holy Spirit revealed my heart is willing to give.
He also revealed that in my heart, I fear
I have not retained all I read in these books,
So I find comfort in having them near—
Somewhat of a security blanket,
Yet God wants me to trust Him completely.
What was fed to my spirit
Is what will come out when needed...now I see.
It's a matter of walking by faith to a greater degree.
The books are tools God used to help me.
The Holy Spirit will pluck up the pages needed by me
As I share Jesus for all to see.
Whether the words are quoted from God's Word
Or the books I've read, or perhaps a song or two—

Maybe a poem as well—
God knows how to cause it to surface for you.
I'm just the vessel.
He's what flows through.
I give Him glory and thank Him for much grace
So I can do what He's asked me to do.

The books will be given to abused women's shelters.
I pray they don't get dusty because they aren't being read.
I pray many people are touched and healed by Jesus
As wisdom and understanding flow to their hearts
And their heads.

7.27.03
Luke 6:38: "Give, and it shall be given unto you; good measure, pressed down, and shaken together, and running over, shall men give into your bosom. For with the same measure that ye mete withal it shall be measured to you again."

FYI: I wrote and published a book telling how I learned to recognize abusive behavior and how to deal with it effectively, God's way: *The Agonized Heart...No More!*

58

Did You Forget?

~⁀

Just as I was comfortably in bed,
This is what I heard:
"Did you forget?"
I said, "Forget what?"
"Forget you're through."
"I'm through…no, no, I didn't forget.
Wednesday, three days ago, I finished chemotherapy."
"You're through!"
"Yes, I'm through."
"Linda, you're through!"
Eyes wide open, I said:
**"I'm *through*! I'm *through*! I'm *through*!
Three days ago…I'm *through*
The valley of the shadow of death!"**
☺
I knew children in the house were sleeping,
So I yelled in spirit
Rather than with my natural voice.
As I did so, I saw the valley rise to meet me
Like a huge hammock being tightened.
The deep dip was removed.
Everything was back on even keel.

No longer was I in the valley of the shadow of death.
God honored His words to me!

The evening prior to learning I faced lung cancer
and surgery,
Followed by radiation and chemotherapy treatments...
When I'd said, "Lord, what *about* all of this?"
Immediately I'd received this *rhema* word:
"It won't be easy, but I will stand beside you
Every step of the way, and I will see you through."
Then He gave me Psalms 23: "Yea, though I walk through
The valley of the shadow of death..."
I knew I would live and not die.
That was followed by lung surgery on March 5, 2003.
This is August 10, 2003. I didn't forget.
As far as circumstances,
I have eighty dollars to my name
After double-tithing as God told me to
For this year, 2003.
If I move in August as planned,
There will be no other designated income
Except from previously sown seed...
That harvest, I have to look forward to.
So what to do?
The pastor asks, "How many people will give fifty dollars
Toward the kids' ministry?"
They needed fifty people.
My hand went up without effort on my part.
My stomach kind of got tight momentarily.
I made a quick calculation.
$100 income, $10 tithe, $10 TV ministry, $50 Kids' Planet

$30 left to go; sixteen hundred miles to Canada this month.
I thought, "The seed does not meet my need,
So, I sow what I have and trust God."
I said, "Lord, my need does not move you,
But my *seed* does…"
I had hardly said it
When I felt the seed plucked
Out of my hand
And already placed in the soil.
I then said,
"I expect a hundredfold harvest

Before the end of August 2003."
Is that ordering God? Hmmmmm—no, that is *faith*!
Can't please God without it! ☺

8.10.03
Malachi 3:10–11; Luke 6:38; Philippians 4:19

P.S. Guess what? On August 27, 2003, I finally flew back to Canada from Texas with my free airline ticket!
(**You can never outgive God, and God will never be indebted to you.** He keeps the books and is accurate to the penny and in all areas. After all, He's perfect.)

P.P.S. Even though at this time, I was bald and extremely weak, the passion of a soul-winner was within me, so I would stay in bed as late as possible to preserve strength while simultaneously looking forward to going to the parks with an evangelistic team. I had changed churches and was impressed with The new church's outreach for youth. I made a commitment to participate twelve evenings throughout the summer. God supernaturally strengthened me to attend each time. I had the honor of giving the altar call to a lot of children and some adults, too, as I stood in the hot Texas sun—and I won't forget the Texas winds, either.

That is why I wore my wig and a scarf...just in case...☺. Those were highlights that kept me going when the going got the roughest. The children's beaming faces became etched in my mind as medicine for my soul and cherished memories. They were the launching pad for me and my final duty as a kickoff to Canada. All in God's perfect timing—glory to God for His faithfulness to me. When God can use someone as weak as I was in such a precious way, He can use anyone. He just needs his or her willingness and passion for the lost.

59

Dear Doctor

~

GOD USED ME in a way I did not expect. I think He likes pulling off surprises. The Holy Spirit told me to write a particular doctor a letter and be like an arrow pointing him to Jesus concerning a problem he had. I wrote and let him know he had helped a lot of people, but God wanted to help him. He needed healing. I spoke of the importance of breaking generational curses and made mention of the pain he was in and the fact that his next generation would have the same problem. I prayed his heart would be touched to read in writing that God wanted to help him. Surely everyone would like to receive a truth like that in writing! Also, I gave him scriptures and the name of a book and a ministry that could help him in this area particularly if he so chose.

Sometimes it feels like God throws a curveball because what He asks us to do is unexpected, but He knows how to get messages to people. The Holy Spirit impressed in my heart that I need not make an office appointment to get the letter to the doctor, but that I was to give it to him personally. That puzzled me because he was so busy our paths might not cross, but I prepared the letter in anticipation.

As I was leaving on my final day of doctor appointments, with the letter in hand, I met the doctor walking down the hall toward me, and I simply handed the letter to him—no fuss. God brought him right to me, and the message was delivered. God knows who He wants, where, and when, and I am really learning not to take such chance meetings for granted but to ask God His purpose in the "divine appointments." They are not coincidences.

There was another person God had me address in writing, and that, too, was unexpected. She was someone who had been a great inspiration to me when I was the sickest and had to be admitted to hospital for nearly a week. Yet there was an area of her life where God wanted to get her attention and bring change, so I brought light to that area with a personal poem to her, followed by a letter of exhortation. She did her job, and I was just doing mine. Again, it was when I was full of chemo and radiation, yet God helped me get the letter done and deliver it, too. It amazes me how all He needs is a willing vessel, because I surely did not feel or look like God could use me for anything, but He did.

Then it made me wonder how many other people He had asked to witness to this person about a certain situation, and they did not let their light shine. At least I know I do not have her blood on my hands if she does not go the route God is asking her to go. That is what each person will one day have to do when his or her day comes...find out if he or she has anyone's blood on his or her hands because he or she denied God and became a people pleaser rather than a God pleaser. If we deny Jesus, He will deny us before the Father. That I do know is truth, because it is the Word of God. I pray we do the right thing always and serve God with our whole hearts. I also pray He keeps preparing us for divine appointments and puts His words in our mouths. He is faithful, but are we?

Isaiah 51:16: "And I have put my words in thy mouth, and I have covered thee in the shadow of mine hand, that I may plant the heavens, and lay the foundations of the earth, and say unto Zion, Thou art my people."

60

Do I or Don't I?

I do. I do write the truth.
So, to omit negative things that occurred
Would be like painting a picture
That is blurred.

Consequently, I will tell you all—
Not in any effort to condemn, for sure,
But to help you see the spiritual viewpoint
Of what I've had to endure:

I witnessed a nurse change the dressing
On another chemo patient's main line
Then leave the room
Like everything was fine.

She did not disinfect the area.
She did not use the swabs from the kit.
The patient complained to another nurse.
I nearly had a fit.

The dressing was redone—
This time properly.
Staph infection is no fun.
I know because it happened to me.

When a lack of integrity is shown
By behavior such as this,
The patient is the one
Who is at risk.

The nurse was spoken to about it all.
I pray she be more diligent in answering her call.
Were doing a job "as unto the Lord,"
She'd be less likely to fall.

It just shows that the patient,
No matter how sick he or she may be,
Must keep alert as much as possible
To keep getting healthier.

Another nurse lied to me twice
By telling me not to come until Tuesday.
Doctor's orders called for me to come
Monday, Wednesday, and Friday,
Yet no copy of orders was given for me to see, no way.

I waited, yet the nurse acted like she was too busy.
Blood is to be drawn on alternate days, so I'm told.

So, this messed me up in getting my cell count up
As well as the scheduled scan, so I'll be bold.

I'll confront the nurse who lied to me twice—
Let her know I know and do not appreciate it at all.
I'm also debating on whether or not
The doctor to call.

My flesh does not like getting involved.
It is easier to sweep it under the rug, for sure,
Than to confront and expose darkness—
Yet it is me having to endure.

That's why when mud comes my way,
I will with righteous indignation use holy boldness,
Because the nurse wasn't fearful as she boldly lied for
the devil.
She started this mess.

There's a saying here: "Don't mess with Texas."
Well, I've got one, too:
**"Don't mess with me, God's child,
Because you're playing with fire when you do!"**

When you mess with me, you're touching God's anointed.
That's a fact.
So, I suggest you pray
Rather than attempting a devious attack.
I spoke the truth,

Yet this little story, my flesh did not want to tell.
It is part of what I experienced, though;
So, I wrote in case you need to—So, you'll sound the bell.

It helps when God's viewpoint is seen,
Not just what's seen with the eyes naturally.
Everyone is in a spiritual battle
And needs eyes to see supernaturally.

8.15.03
Revelation 2:7: "He that hath an ear, let him hear what the Spirit saith unto the churches; To him that overcometh will I give to eat of the tree of life, which is in the midst of the paradise of God."

61

Luggage Anyone?

~⌒

Not once but many times today,
Jesus revealed Himself to me.
How do I know it was Jesus?
The presence of Jesus is not duplicated
By any other presence.

For example:
After many people had been praying
The perfect will of God for me,
With regard to getting a scan done—
As it had been postponed six times—
Today was the day I would learn
If I had a green light to get it done
Or not.

I had favor everywhere I went:
Half the parking lot was closed.
I prayed for a convenient parking spot.
Got one closest to the door
Then learned the doctor was at the hospital,
Yet he was not gone long at all.
He scheduled the scan for tomorrow.

I received my medical records.
The twenty-five-dollar fee was waived.

Then I was told the main line comes out today!
When we were waiting to get it done,
In walked a new chemo-patient friend.
She volunteered to drive me to the appointment
For my scan tomorrow,
Yet she would not get her blood work done today
As she was taking a friend for lunch.
So she rescheduled...which means
God led her there to meet my need tomorrow:
It was a divine appointment.

Then I met another chemo patient and
Shared testimony with her.
She was happy for me.
The main line was removed
Without pain, thankfully.
I bid the chemo room and friends
Farewell with mixed emotions.
I sowed a lot of seeds in that room,
Ministering to patients and staff
About Jesus and His love and
The fact that a right relationship with God
Will bring you through any trial.
Tears were shed in that room.
Fear was battled in that room.
Laughter and joy filled that room.
Love was manifested in that room.

God was there all the time.
The memories are priceless.

Upon leaving I hugged some nurses
And the receptionist, who created the book
To house my poetry, as well as that of others.
When I reached the front door of the hospital,
I felt like weights were lifting off me.
I had been there twice today:
Once at 8:30 a.m. to get lab work done.
And then to pick up my medical records
Plus all my x-rays (sixteen pounds).
Today was graduation day for sure.
But that is not all that happened.

Friends where I live took me out to dinner.
Then they bought me a piece of luggage with wheels.
That was an answer to prayer, as it met a need.
Then I phoned my ride for tomorrow.
In the course of the conversation, I asked

If she knew anyone that might want a garment bag
And a duffel bag
In place of one large piece of luggage.
It was a long shot,
But I thought to myself,
"You never know who might have said to her
Even one week ago
That they had no room for a big piece of luggage
And did not know what to do with it."

Sure enough, she said, "Yes, I have one!"
She proceeded to tell me that a new water heater
Had been installed in her large walk-in closet
At the apartment where she lives.
Consequently, her "large piece of luggage"
Was sitting in the bedroom with no home.
We were both laughing and somewhat in awe.

Our God is an awesome God.
He supplies every need.
Then I had a chance to share some pertinent facts
That will help her to be alert
As she walks through this valley.
She knows what to look for and to be prepared.
It was good that my recent experience
Could help her, and that blessed and encouraged me.
She also told me that she had never seen a chemo patient
With such good color as I had.

I just had to tell her the importance of reading the Word of
God.
When you put light in,
Light comes out.
That's just a fact.
You cannot be full of the Word of God
And have it not show.
Time must be spent with Him to change.

All in all, I would say
It's been another good day
Because I recognize the hand of God in my life

So many times as He makes Himself real to me.
All I did was flow with the Holy Spirit
And let it all happen.
God sure does have a good plan.
He looks after every detail.
Imagine that…He even cares about
Luggage.

He also cares whether or not
We have any excess spiritual baggage.
He does not overlook anything.
He's a God who cannot fail.
When is the last time
He revealed Himself to you?
Think about it.
I pray the Holy Spirit will show you
As you wait in His presence,
Because He is no respecter of persons.
What He wants to show you is good.
So, relax and rest in His presence
As you listen to His small, still voice—
So strong, yet so gentle.
His sheep know His voice.
Listen carefully:
He is talking to you.
Yes, you! ☺

John 10:3: "To him the porter openeth; and the sheep hear his voice: and he calleth his own sheep by name, and leadeth them out."

FYI: My chemo buddy who provided the luggage is now in heaven. (That makes seven.) I look forward to seeing her again someday, too, but we won't need our luggage.

62

Graduation Day for Me

~~

Why was that my graduation day?
That was the day the blessed main line was removed
From my chest after four months.
It did a lot of good
Because I did not have to get individual needles,
Yet in other ways it was such a thorn—
Making it difficult to get comfortable
When I lay on my side or stomach.
Yet it was most necessary to be there,
So I call it another case of
Enduring a bit of long-suffering;
Yet it was not anything at all
Compared to the suffering Jesus did for me.

I find it interesting that just tonight,
I watched a woman on TV
Share testimony of her experience with cancer
In the last three months' time.
She elected not to have chemotherapy.
Her journey has been difficult,
Including colon surgery,
Whereas I had lung surgery;

Yet she is doing just fine,
And so am I.

I had tears as a song was sung.
Dean and Mary Brown sang
"Pick Up Your Faith."
I cried as the Lord touched me
From deep within.
I cried some more—
Knew there was a release.

God revealed some things to me.
It really was quite a night—
Quite a successful night.
God touched me,
And I knew I'd be all right.

8.20.03
Psalms 41:11: "By this I know that thou favourest me,
because mine enemy doth not triumph over me."

63

Life in the Fast Lane

~~

I take one long look at the plains of Amarillo, Texas,
As I watch the airplanes leave the runway,
Lifting off into the blue sky.
This fine day of August 27, 2003, has finally arrived.
Soon it will be me
Who is lifting off, too.
My family will meet me in Toronto.
They are excited, too.
It has been nearly three years
Since I've been back home.
This time it is much more than a visit.
I am going home not to die,
But to live!

Circumstances may not appear as such,
As for the first time in my life,
I am in a wheelchair.
My body is full of chemo and radiation,
So I have no strength and no immune system.
I am not in the granny lane, though;
I found out there is a perk to this chair...
As I was escorted to the plane in

The fast lane!

That is how some people live:
Swerving from one lane to the next
Without hesitation, fearlessly,
Seemingly without thinking at all.
Yet with each mile behind them,
They are closer to their ultimate destination—
Either heaven or hell.
I observed many people today
At the Dallas airport—
People of all races

Rushing to and fro.
My thoughts were about salvation.
I wondered which way they would go
If today was their day.
As the eyes are the mirror
To the soul, there were times
I knew if the person was born again.
By now I am familiar with the inner witness
The Holy Spirit has given me
After serving the Lord Jesus Christ for twenty-five years.
Consequently, I also observed
The lack of the fear of the Lord in many people.
To have the fear of the Lord is the beginning of wisdom.
Though the crowds were orderly,
The atmosphere was somehow tense.
I suspect many had thoughts of 9/11,
Though they were not verbalized.
Perhaps others were merely overwhelmed

By the vastness of the airport.
In fact, I was in awe
As I've only flown four times—
In awe of the size of the airport
And the smoothness with which my trip went.
To a *T*, as they say.
Praise the Lord; safety is of Him—
Romans 8:28, too, as good came out of this.
Those in wheelchairs get escorted
To the fast lane,
And I know the final destination for me
Is heaven for eternity!

8.27.03
Proverbs 9:10, 11: "The fear of the Lord is the beginning of wisdom: and the knowledge of the holy is understanding. For by me thy days shall be multiplied, and the years of thy life shall be increased."

64

All about Life

~⌒

Life brings changes.
Time brings changes.
Illness brings changes.
Decisions bring changes.
Seasons bring changes.
So, get used to it.
Change is necessary.
The greater the change,
The greater the opportunity—
Opportunity for growth and development.
Heat brings change to cake batter.
Transition takes place.
The results reflect the change.
Next comes the icing on the cake:
A smooth, soothing application,
Causing the appearance to be changed considerably.
Amazing what a little color can do—
And a few roses, strategically placed.

When the Holy Spirit paints a picture,
The anointing rests
As an unmistakable presence

Causing the icing on the cake,
So to speak, to be sweeter than sweet.
It becomes something beautiful indeed—
From glory to glory, which is good
Because that is what these changes are all about:
Life!

9.14.03
FYI: This was written in Ontario, Canada. I made it back finally!

John 10:10: "The thief cometh not, but for to steal, and to kill, and to destroy: I am come that they might have life, and that they might have it more abundantly."

65

Make My Day

~~~

People are praying for me.
God is lifting me up.
I feel it from deep within.
Transition time has filled my cup.
There are lots of changes to experience
When moving sixteen hundred miles away
To Ontario, Canada, from Texas, United States.
I've been writing lots of letters.
That is something I *can* do.
Getting all of my books published
Is something else I want to do.
There is a time and a season for everything, though.
I realize I must be patient and stay in the flow
Of God's Spirit everywhere I go.
Whether I am at Walmart, the bank, or a restaurant,
My eyes are on Jesus, and with Him I commune
Morning, night, and noon.
He is with me 24-7.
What more can I say?
To you, it may sound religious.
To me, that makes my day.
Think about it.

How many unanswered phone calls have you made?
How frustrated did you get?
If you would have called on Jesus first,
There'd be no unanswered calls yet.
Jesus won't make you stand in line.
Jesus won't put you on hold.
When Jesus answers your call,
His voice is like pure liquid gold.
Your heart and your ears perk up.
You embrace each word you hear.
When Jesus speaks, He *says* something.
With him, there is no fear.
No wonder he makes my day.
He doesn't love me more than you.
Will you call on Jesus, please?
He'll make your day, too!

9.20.03
His phone number is Jeremiah 33:3: "Call unto me, and I will answer thee, and show thee great and mighty things, which thou knowest not."

66

Any Foundation Problems?

My prayer is for God to reveal
Any problems in my foundation.
As I arose this morning
And sat in my chair
With my Bible before me,
I kept sensing God's presence.
Then I saw the face of someone praying.
He was praying for me.
Tears came to my eyes.
He has so much to do,
Yet he takes time to pray for me.
It makes me want to pray more
So he won't have to.
I know it is a spiritual battle—
Severe at this time—
But no matter the height or fierceness of the waves,
My God always protects me and always makes a way.

Little is much when God is in it.
He has undergirded my faith recently.
My hand is in His, and He orders my steps.

He keeps reminding me of the deep, deep valley
He brought me through...

10.2.03
Psalms 37:23: "The steps of a good man are ordered by the Lord: and he delighteth in his way."

67

Praise the Lord!

~

Taking your next breath
Can't be taken for granted,
Whether you've had lung surgery
Or not.
It is easy to assume
The next breath is there for the taking.
In fact, most people breathe
Without even wondering if...
The next breath is there,
Ready and waiting.
So in case you
Have taken many breaths for granted...

11.15.03
How about doing as Psalms 150:6 says? "Let every thing that hath breath praise the Lord. Praise ye the Lord."

68

Not Left Out, Just Left Last!

~~~

Initial Symptoms and Addressing Stress

THE DOCTOR SAID **the cancer was caused by** *stress.* As I had divorced five months before finding the tumor, the doctor's diagnosis was right on. I emerged from an abusive relationship and wrote a book about my experiences: *The Agonized Heart...No More.* It is available from Amazon.com and other retailers. The divorce was finalized a few weeks after 9/11. Just five months later, I had lung surgery.

If you are reading this book in sequence, you will notice a few loose ends; it was not written in sequence because the more chemo I received during the writings, the more my memory was affected. I did not realize it at first, and I was not told it would be expected.

My memory did recover in time, but it was alarming to realize there were blank spots at first. I had to make a determined effort not to fear the loss and not to get stressed trying to make myself remember things. Rather, I tried to just deal with it as a side effect and pray for restoration. Now, if I do not remember something, my excuse is "That was BC" (before chemo!). Also, after the treatments were done, it was important to use a lot of vitamins to help rebuild my immune system.

When I think about a reader's perspective, I realize questions will come up, such as "Did you smoke? What were the symptoms?" I could tell you in a few sentences, but as a writer, it is important for me to help you get a true perspective of the situation, and to do so, I must be specific and release from a transparent heart painful experiences—yet I am not looking back. I am through, as stated previously. **Let's begin with the cause of the cancer: stress.**

The word *stress* could mean something very different to different individuals if they were to define their level of tolerance. Let's just say the stress I endured was not just that of an abusive relationship followed by a divorce. Here are a few samples of what I experienced in the short five-month time frame between the divorce's becoming final and my receiving the horrific diagnosis. My reason for sharing this is to show others that no matter how many Goliaths they face, they can overcome if they become changed on the inside with God's help to transform, renew, and restore. It is a process, as is salvation. "Work out your own salvation with fear and trembling." Philippians 2:12

In becoming more Christlike, I learned to deal with stress, not sweep it under the rug or go into denial. Whether the Goliath I faced was stress, fear, manipulation, intimidation, control, cancer, jealousy, anger, religious spirits, carnality—whatever!—I learned to face it head on. As I share, you will see why it is so important to be led by the Holy Spirit rather than by emotions, carnal thinking, or religious mind-sets.

Religion did not help me one bit. A personal relationship with Jesus Christ is how I overcame, and the roots were strong because I stayed close to Him and His

Word, no matter what any Goliath said or did. The Lord helped me to mature spiritually, stay focused, develop stronger muscles to soar far higher than an eagle, yet dig deeper than ever before as I serve in His army. The longer I serve Him, the more I overcome in Christ. Hopefully you won't have to face symptoms such as I did a few weeks before seeing the doctor.

I was almost asleep when I heard myself wheeze. It startled me so much, I was wide awake. I knew it was not my imagination, and it definitely bothered me—but not enough that I went to the doctor. I made the mistake of playing doctor—not good. The body is created to give warning signs when something is wrong. It was definitely a red flag. As I had not smoked in over twenty-five years, the wheeze alarmed me. God delivered me from nicotine instantly, before I was saved. God delivered me from nicotine addiction on June 11, 1978, instantly. I looked up at the sky and said, "God, if You are really real, will You please help me quit smoking, because I can't do it myself?"

I admit that it was hardly a faith-filled prayer. Nevertheless, I woke up the following Sunday morning not smoking and not wanting a cigarette. The Holy Spirit wooed me for four months into a personal, lifelong commitment on October 22, 1978! God is more than faithful, whatever you call that! Back to the wheezing incident.

A week or so later, it happened again. This time I got upset and also realized there had been times at work when my equilibrium had been off. Also, I would have a day when instantly I would be absolutely exhausted and weak for no apparent reason, yet I kept working. As I sold furniture in a huge warehouse and walked all day long, it was easy to earmark those experiences. Unfortunately, I did not tie them together, which is why I say, "Do not play doctor. Let the doctor do his or her job. Just be the patient and go." Time was—and is—ticking.

As well as working full time, I was busy moving in to my own apartment. Moving everything from the large storage building was quite a chore in the hot weather. Help was scarce, so I did most of it myself. Even though I had given away all the furniture, I was excited to have my own home again after living with other families from various churches for over a year.

God restored me mentally, emotionally, physically, and spiritually during that time frame. I applied for jobs but did not get hired even though I was willing to work. God is a God of order, and He had a plan. He used me in each home in ways I never would have expected. It was a two-way street. God was there, too.

My plan was to move back to Ontario, Canada (I had moved to Texas, United States, and lived there about twelve years), but I did not have the money to get back home. When my ex-husband filed for divorce, the Lord simply said, **"Don't fight."** So, I let go of five acres and a new home; everything, except the furniture I was given. I said, "Lord, there isn't enough to fight over anyway, and You are my provider, so I will put my trust in You."

In the middle of all of this, as people blessed me by welcoming me into their homes, God blessed them for helping me. I saw what happened to those who did as unto the Lord. Yet my home church at the time kicked me out because they said living with other people like I did brought reproach to the Lord. Yet they helped me one time financially when I leased the apartment. I will point out what happened to the first family that took me in so I did not have to go to a hospital because of the extreme exhaustion.

God showed me that He was going to bless them in a special way for helping me. I did not know how, but I knew when it happened, they would know why they'd been so blessed, and I told them so. They were given $10,000 cash, no strings, just two weeks after I moved out. I was there just under five months. The church that kicked me out had nothing to say about that testimony, though.

Oh, how sad when religious spirits interfere with God's plan, which is so perfect. One of the other families that took me in were the ones I gave most of the furniture to, so God blessed them as well. Other families also helped and were blessed. The church had no comment about those testimonies. I am so glad my focus was on the Lord because He just kept healing my spirit from the wounds it received from carnal religious mind-sets.

For example, I was told my old pickup did not look good out front in the church parking lot and that I could park at the back. Well, I had a different viewpoint, and so did God. As I attended virtually every service and always went early, I parked where it was convenient, which was at the front, near the door. When I drove my brand-new Cougar, no one complained about me parking out front. Well, the Cougar, the house, and the husband were all gone, and I still attended church.

When I moved into town and called six people to get a ride, none of them was going to the midweek service. I was surprised. I had not...lost my zeal! I prayed and told God if He wanted me to go to church, I needed transportation.

Long story short, I went to one of the home Bible study groups, and someone at that group told me, "You need a vehicle, and I *have* a vehicle!" The gentleman gave me his pickup truck. He also said he'd tried to give it away a few times, but the Lord told him not to give it to the guy who asked. He did not know why until he heard me pray, asking the Lord for transportation so I could get to Bible study. God told him, as I was praying out loud with the group, to give the pickup to me because of my motive. Everyone was rejoicing. I was praying it was *not* a stick shift. It wasn't. See—God knows what is best for me! It was a blue '83 Chevy full-bed pickup, and I was thrilled. God also knew I would need that pickup to move soon. He looks after details when you obey and trust Him.

Funny how certain people find it an eyesore and worry that it will look like the congregation is not prospering if its members drive old vehicles, yet many of the newer ones were not at church. God knows. How many drivers of those vehicles are willing to offer a ride to someone (with a right attitude) and are willing to even go out of their way? I am glad I please God and know not to be a people pleaser, because it is an impossibility if you think you can please everyone. Another thing God knew (as He knows the end from the beginning) was that I was going to be moving to my own apartment and needed the pickup to move my things.

I just had another recollection...one day I called the church, asking if they knew anyone who lived in my area and attended the church as I needed a ride after the marriage broke up. I was told, "We are not running a taxi service here." It was not the answer I expected to hear. I prayed for the staff member, who happened to be a pastor's wife. Sometimes people can make you feel like a thorn, but I remind myself that roses have thorns, and I am determined to keep blossoming while simultaneously reminding myself there is no perfect church.

I also remind myself that I am being perfected, and I am hearing from God, thankfully. In fact, I remember thinking when the comment entered my ear, "Lord, did You hear that?" **(I wanted to tell Him to plug his ears because I knew it was the wrong thing to say to me or to anyone.) What if that had been Jesus needing a ride?**

Please don't waste time trying to figure out which church did this, because that is not important. Learn from my experience. Get your eyes open to see spiritually, recognize manipulation and control, and check the fruit. No church is perfect, yet it is necessary to remove the log in one's own eye before trying to remove the speck in someone else's eye. For example, a pastor told someone I was supposed to be living in Canada and not even be at the church yet did not inform me. When I said I did not have the funds to go back but wanted to, I was told it was my fault because I had not saved.

I let it be known that I was not on commission—salary only. This was a shock to my accuser, proving I had been judged incorrectly. How easy it is to point fingers—and how damaging, too. **I was actually happier with my old pickup, my little apartment with no furniture, and my job selling furniture than others were who had far more materially and financially.**

My heart held my treasures—an intimate, growing relationship with Jesus—and no one could rob me of that

blessing! God healed my broken heart, but stress was taking its toll, unbeknownst to me at the time. (X-rays proved the tumor grew within an eight-month period.)

You may wonder how I managed in an apartment with no furniture. Do you think God has a sense of humor to give me a job selling and dusting beautiful furniture only to go home to my apartment with no furniture? I was coming home to boxes covered with blankets and lace cloths—but there was love in that home. Besides, lovely furnishings do not make a house a home. Now I had wall-to-wall boxes of all the other things that you box up when moving, so I lined up some boxes and put a blanket over them against one wall; then I put the stereo and a lamp and a clock on top. It became a bookcase headboard for the bed. Who knew? Only me. I was given a metal frame and mattress and box spring, so that worked great. The first two nights I slept on the floor with a sleeping bag, but it was still great to be in my own place, and I was able to praise the Lord in the midst of all the boxes.

I set up my computer; that is a must! A new neighbor gave me a wooden door, which became the desktop. Boxes under either end became the pedestal, covered with a color-ful tablecloth, and it worked fine. Necessity is the mother of invention. I like interior decorating, so I had my work cut out. It was an opportunity for creativity to blossom. It had to because I did not have funds to purchase furniture, nor did I want to because I planned on moving back to Canada. *But God* knew some things I didn't, and thankfully, He had a plan.

I had lived in my apartment for over four months when my faith was sorely tried in another area—or should I say I encountered some stress! Another long story short (which is nearly impossible for me to do) is that I quit my job. My boss told me that if a customer sneezed, and I said, "God bless you," I would be fired. (It is better to offend the boss than offend Jesus, and I knew my priorities.) I met the owner and told him to his face exactly that truth, and I quit without hesitation or fear, although he tried three times to get me to go inside and talk. I had heard from God and knew not to compromise. (I have learned the owner has since passed after a battle with cancer.)

Sometimes we are tested to see if our trust is in a paycheck or in God to provide. To line up another job first would mean looking at the paycheck as the source, even though to our natural minds, it sounds logical. (Becoming a supernatural person is not necessarily logical, but it is God's way.) Taking a stand when the issue presents itself is when it is time to do so—not at my convenience. I do not need the security blanket of the next job when I have my trust in the Lord.

As I drove home, I said, "Lord, you are my spiritual husband, and we need to pay the rent. Thank you for being a good provider." Then I visited a Christian friend and kind of shook her up with my unexpected news. She asked, "What are you going to do?" I said, "I am going to go home and praise the Lord. He gave me the courage to quit and not compromise."

The rent was paid anonymously, praise God. Meanwhile, I got to know the neighbors across the hall and another family on another floor of my apartment building. The second family was able to use a lot of things I did not need and had doubles of things like dishes and such. They had previously lost their house in a fire, so it was a thrill to be able to bless them as well as become good friends. There are no coincidences with God. I saw His hand at work. I witnessed to a neighbor about tithing and how God had blessed me in so many ways over the years. The next thing I knew, she came to my door and handed me a check, explaining that she wanted to tithe, and because I had taught her, she gave it to me.

I accepted it on that principle but told her that next time, it should go to her home church. She came to the door a second time within a few weeks with another check for me. I declined. She adamantly explained that she had gotten a totally unexpected check in the mail from her insurance company and was giving me the tithe from it. After that she would give her tithe to her church because she knew tithing works! I accepted—but not after that day. She knew God moved on her behalf and that He was calling her to tithe. So her "proof tithe" proved He honors tithing, and she became committed financially as well as with her heart. It was exciting to see the Holy Spirit move in her life and that of her family. God knows how to touch hearts and woo lovingly.

The end of December arrived, and my lease had expired; plus, I was not employed. My time was spent writing, studying, and witnessing. Then a family invited me to move in with them and insisted I take the master bedroom. Everyone was in agreement, so just before Christmas, I did exactly that, as I did not have the money to go back to Canada. My boxes were moved to a smaller storage building, and I got settled with my new family.

Things were fine until I started getting a terrible headache. It became a migraine (I had never had one in my life) after three days, and I had to go to the hospital. They took x-rays, and when the doctor stood by my side in the emergency room, I knew when I looked at his face that he felt sorry for me. He knew something but was not telling me—that, I *did* know. He simply said, "You need to see your family doctor. The x-ray showed a spot at the tip of your lung." My first thought was "I hope I don't have TB." He also said there was a bit of arthritis at the tip of my neck. My mind told me this was why I had the headache pain—arthritis.

I went to the doctor, and when he picked up my file, he got so nervous he dropped it. He left the room momentarily, and I wondered what was wrong. He returned, handed me a business card, and told me he had made an appointment with a surgeon whom I needed to talk to. I thought, "Why a surgeon? I'm not having surgery." He did not tell me what was wrong.

Although I do not remember exactly when this next incident happened, I will not ever forget it. I went to bed, was lying on my tummy, and pushed with my hands and arms to roll over, but something hurt. I lay flat on my tummy again, raised up, and felt the soreness again. It was not my imagination. I examined my breasts, and there was no lump and no tenderness. It was a relief because the discomfort was very real.

Again, I lay on my tummy and raised up, placing two fingers where the tenderness was. It did not hurt when I pressed in. Then I discovered the pain occurred when I lifted my weight up away from the mattress. This puzzled me. It was like touching a bruise, but the pain was not felt when you touched it. The pain came when your fingers departed from the bruise. I knew for sure something was *very* wrong, and part of me just froze.

The night before the appointment with the surgeon was the night I simply said, "What *about* all of this, Lord?"

Immediately He said, **"It won't be easy, but I will stand beside you every step of the way, and I will see you through."**

I wept and wept. I was thankful for the answer, but it was not the answer I wanted to hear. As I believe in healing, and God had healed my shoulder miraculously of a calcium deposit years before, I believed in healing at this time also. But God did not say, "On such and such a date, your healing will be manifested." I did not let myself think any further. I actually went to sleep.

The next day a friend went with me to the surgeon's office. When he spoke the word *tumor*, I think everything seemed like it was in slow motion from that point on because he'd said there was a tumor in my lung. He showed me the x-ray, and I was horrified. It was bigger than a golf ball, smaller than a baseball. I wanted to flick it away from the tip of my lung, but I couldn't.

It made me feel so invaded, so overtaken by this foreign thing inside my body. I was repulsed, yet what could I do? Crying did not happen. I was too stunned. His lips moved, and he spoke, but I don't think I heard anything because as I stood looking at the x-ray, it actually helped me *not* to go into denial.

He handed me a book the size of a comic book, showing the surgery step by step with photos. It took me a week to get through that book, especially the part that said the doctor breaks a few ribs to get to the lung. Just thinking about that hurt! I was glad the incision was not at the front but at my side and upward on my back. Yet it was gruesome to read about—or should I say stressful?

During that time period, my daughter flew in from Canada. We cried together and had to deal with issues such as my will, and what if: what to do, where I would be buried, the funeral, what hymns to sing…all of it. We covered the gamut. We faced the issues head on and painfully, with even some laughter to break the tension at one point when I said, "Pull the plug!" It was a precious time of bonding together—yet stressful to say the least.

Surgery was scheduled quickly, and I was admitted with total peace, yet because it happened so fast, I wondered if I was in shock because I had so much peace. I decided peace was good, so I just did what was necessary, and there truly was no fear. **Hearing from God that special night was the knot in the end of the rope I hung on to, and I did not let go—ever!** One of the last forms I had to fill out before surgery was for donor information, and it upset me to find out I could not donate my eyes if they found cancer. I could not be a donor. It was upsetting because I had always wanted to do that if need be. Another disappointment to deal with… or was it stress?

Okay, that is a peek through a small window of my life prior to the actual surgery. All that stress was in a five-month period, and there was even more; but I am publishing more books, so check my website regularly at www.lindaloujones.com, please.

On March 5, 2003, right after I came out of surgery, my daughter excitedly told me that my brother and my son-in-law (her husband) had driven down from Ontario, Canada, and were surprising me with a visit. She said they had driven the twenty-five-hour trip straight through to see me and would be there any minute.

What was meant to be a blessing almost backfired because I thought that for the two men to drive straight through must have meant they were in such a hurry because I was going to die! I was horrified and asked my daughter, **"Am I going to** *die*?" **She quickly scooted around the bed and assured me that was not the case! Talk about trauma on top of surgery!** ☺

Incredibly, it was about ten minutes after the surgeon told me they'd found cancer that my family arrived. God's timing is perfect. When you need someone to hold your hand, He'll work it all out. **As for the other times you *think* you need someone, just hold more tightly onto Jesus's hand. You won't hear Him complain. In fact, He likes holding hands. I know!** ☺

This brings you up to the first entry in the book: "Me… or…God *in* Me." It was written three weeks after the lung surgery, so I guess this is full circle. My prayer is that you are touched deeply by God as you read these words: *Scalpel to Sword*. Also I pray that you are greatly encouraged and challenged to become more like Christ, whether you are a cancer patient, a cancer survivor, a relative or friend of someone with cancer, a person who has lost someone to cancer, or someone who simply needs a special touch from God. I pray God uses this book mightily to remove fear, replace it with hope, and kindle a bright flame of passion for Christ in you from head to toe—because no matter what the battle, a right relationship with God will see you through!

You do not have to ever be alone. Jesus loves you, and only Jesus saves. Love Him back. **Trust Him to see you through.** He loves you so much. I pray Calvary was not in vain. The closer you stay to the Master, the deeper your roots will be. When the storms come, you will remain intact. It is not complicated. True—the road is narrow, and there is a price to pay, but Jesus is the only way; so why not just pray and obey? It works!

Bottom line: I have been cancer-free over fourteen years now! Glory to God! ☺ **I couldn't wait to tell you this, but keep reading: the steak is coming, too. Prophecy is being fulfilled, as you will read in the next entry.**

69

It Is My Timing Now

~

The windows of heaven are open.
You have given much.
I am giving much.
I honor My Word.
You are about to reap
What you sowed.
It is My timing
For restoration to you
In every area of your life.
I honor your obedience,
Your commitment, your trust in Me;
Your faithfulness, pure heart, and clean hands;
Your loyalty and integrity.
You are a virtuous woman,
A lady with much to offer,
For out of your pure heart
Flows a river of life
That is pure, wholesome, and
With a never-ending supply.
As you stay in the flow
Of My Spirit,

Much joy there will be in your life
As you reach out to help others.
You are My vessel, prepared for service,
And I am sending you forth...
A *sent one*...
All over the world
To share My love, compassion, and truth:
My Word, My Son's Calvary victory.
And as you share freely,
Others will see and know you speak
Words of life, truth, and love.
They will want what you have:

A relationship with your Savior and Lord
That is personal and pure.
So *go forth*,
Be led by My Spirit—
Here, there, and everywhere.
You will circulate among the elite,
As well as those who have lost much,
Bringing encouragement and hope.
For you will be to them
As a bright light at the end of a dark tunnel,
Or as a rainbow in the sky
After the storm has passed,
Symbolizing the love and promise of My presence.
I love you, My daughter,
My sister, My friend, My bride.
Continue, in the vine, to abide.
Freely you have given; freely you shall receive.

Freely you have received; freely give. ☺ ☺ ☺
Much unconditional love I give to you.
Your Heavenly Father, Jesus, the Holy Spirit.
"Christ...in you, the hope of glory." ☺

12.12.02 is when I wrote the above piece. This is 12.07.17.
The Holy Spirit told me to place it here at the **end** of the book, even though it was written **before** all other entries. I asked, "Why?"

He said, **"Because it was prophetic, and now is the time: manifestation time."** ☺

Is that not awesome indeed? **Wow! I have been gloriously cancer-free for fourteen years and nine months! Very excited to finally publish this book. I do not believe in coincidences. It is a God "instance." His kiss, unmissed, plus divine timing.** Suffice to say God's plan for me is big, and my motto is **"Small world...big God!"** He took me from being cancer-free to a requirement of "death to self." It is a process requiring His help continually.**

I must not forget a prophecy I received from a pastor in Canada nearly one year after I received the above piece. He said that **God is healing me first, and then He will restore in every area of my life—even put steps on the mountain if necessary.** That was very encouraging because it took nearly one year for me to get the chemo out of my system and get my strength back. The winter air made it difficult to breathe, so I had to stay in and did not have the strength to climb a set of stairs. The day I made it to the top stair at the hockey arena to watch my grandson play a game was a milestone. So, it was a gradual restoration. I was given the use of a computer by another pastor and typed for hours every day that first winter, so I have inspired writings to publish. The following poem shows why I am able to recognize God's kisses—spiritual kisses.

Following Jesus

Following Jesus on a daily basis
Means you will do things you did not plan.
You will toss your agenda aside.
You will dare to be different.
You will not care what others think.
You will be separate from the crowd.
You will be constantly swimming upstream.

You will be aware of a deep inner peace.
You will have a confidence that grows,
As will your faith.
You will hear the voice of the Lord.
You will be sensitive not to grieve the Holy Spirit.
You will desire to be sensitive in the presence of the
Lord 24-7.
Your desires will differ from those of many others.

You will keep becoming more Christlike.
You will want to obey.
You will prosper and be in health as your soul prospers.
You will have a burden for souls.
You will have compassion for the hurting.
You will have love for the unlovable.
You will have a love for God's Word.

You will have wisdom and understanding.
You will excel at all you do.
You will be focused.
You will be ready for action.

You will be God's love in action.
Yes,
You!

1.1.03, 3:30 a.m.

"Following Jesus" shows the condition of my heart prior to the cancer diagnosis just eight weeks later. Spiritual roots were evident and were greatly needed and appreciated because the spiritual, mental, and emotional battles were intense, as was the physical battle. To stay in close communion with Jesus is to always have hope in your heart.

Today is 12.07.17, and I have been cancer-free for over fourteen years! Glory to God! He promised to restore my health first and then bring restoration in every other area, and God is faithful.

Thank you for taking time to read *Scalpel to Sword*. My prayer is that your heart is changed for the better as a result because you have eyes to see how to recognize Jesus working in your life on a daily basis. Hunger and thirst for righteousness because He will fill you. Never quit; never give up.

Rather, be a torch and help others get ignited as your heart releases what God has put in you. When the going gets rough, remember: Jesus is closer to you than any problem. He will never leave you or forsake you. Reach out right now. He knows how to make his presence real to you. Love Him back. Serve Him with your whole heart. I pray you discover how much Jesus Christ loves you.

News Flash: The final chapter is not just addressing those who lost someone to cancer as I did. Chapter 70 is hugely important—possibly the most important chapter

of all seventy—because the welcome mat is extended to everyone. **This enables you to receive a huge breakthrough in the spiritual realm as I did if you are willing to receive and recognize a need for change.** I share this incredible truth because I care for souls. I no longer believe a lie; truth has replaced deception because of learning the necessity of "death to self" and how to achieve God's standard for me. It is a process of preparation. Keep in mind that *remnant* means "few."

Initially, this chapter was written to those who lost someone to cancer. However, the Holy Spirit inspired me to write more, and the breakthrough I received in July 2005 has become a pathway for you to receive. God is no respecter of persons. You will be challenged to go much deeper than the surface level of God's Word—much deeper. Thus, the significance of the Sword, in the title 'Scalpel to Sword'. The Sword, the Word of God plunged far deeper than the scalpel.

Truths will be imparted through seed. The Word of God is the seed, the *sperma* Word of God. God will supernaturally impregnate you with the revelatory Word of God so that you may learn the mysteries. **The mysteries are the secret way God governs the righteous, but they are hidden to carnal, wicked, ungodly people.** If your thinking is carnal, you won't get it; so prepare your heart accordingly before reading this last chapter. **You have been called out of religion and carnal interpretations of God's Word. Are you willing to change and receive God's DNA?** Read on: the best is yet to come, and it is scriptural.

70

To Those Who Lost Someone to Cancer

~⌇

Plus: From a Wake Up to a Shake Up and More

THIS IS ESPECIALLY for you if you are a Christian who prayed for an individual to be healed and it did not happen. Death followed. I know exactly how that feels because it happened to me when my father died of cancer after a five-year battle. I had questions and needed answers. Over the years God taught me things that I will now try to impart to you, and I pray it helps. First of all, let me take you to the day I laid hands on my dad at his home, as he sat in a chair, and prayed for him. My daughter and my mother prayed together in agreement with me as we encircled Daddy.

When we stopped praying, he took a big white hanky and wiped the tears off his face. Then he checked his vision. He had been blind in one eye and had worn hearing aids all his life, so I was not praying only about the cancer; I was being specific. Daddy checked his eyes, covering and uncovering them again and again. Finally, he said, "Nothing. Nothing." (This meant the one eye was still blind.) Well, I had only been saved for two years at the time, and even I was surprised at the answer God gave me for him. I said, "That's okay, Daddy. Sometimes it is gradual." He looked directly at me and grabbed on to that hope, saying, "Oh."

When I went home, it troubled me that something was still not right. I knew that Jesus heals because I had received a miraculous healing of a calcium deposit in my shoulder when I had been saved for only four months. Surgery was avoided. God healed me from the inside miraculously. My doctor saw the x-rays before and after the changes and asked me what happened. She stood embracing her clipboard and looked at me very sternly. Excitedly, I told her I was a Christian now and prayed, and Jesus healed me. She would not write it in her report. With holy boldness (because at that time I had been saved four months ago and had been baptized in the Holy Spirit with the evidence one month prior), I said, "Doctor, if I told you I made a poultice of peanut butter and spinach for my shoulder and was healed, would you put that in your report?"

She nodded yes.

I said, **"Well, that is *not* what happened! *Jesus* healed me. Write it down."** She would not, and I left, taking my healing with me! That healing was a stepping-stone in the development of my faith, because three months later, my mom was instantly healed of arthritis when I stood in proxy and prayed for her in agreement with a TV evangelist. She had been bedridden for three months, and God totally healed her as she lay in her bed just two miles down the road from me.

So, when I prayed for Daddy a few years later, it was with every bit of faith I had that I released those prayers. I also supported them with the Word of God, knowing God's Word does not come back void but will accomplish what it is sent to do. No wonder I wondered why Daddy was not yet healed: I did all I had been taught to do, and it had worked for other people, so why not Daddy? It did not seem fair. He did take the Bible off the shelf as God told me he would.

He also prayed one day with a preacher on TV and said to my mother, "I prayed that prayer with that fellow, but I don't feel any different." When my mother told me this by phone, you can imagine I dropped the phone and had a hallelujah hoedown right in the kitchen! I knew for sure Daddy was born again at that point. **However, salvation is a process to be worked out with fear and trembling. God requires much more than a prayer. He requires death to self. Daily.**

A year had passed, with Daddy losing more of his hearing and cancer spreading throughout his body gradually. At this point in my life, I had the opportunity to be discouraged when it came to praying for healing. I knew it wasn't the prayer that was the problem. It was something else. Besides, Jesus is the healer anyway, not me, so I had to keep praying while also thinking, "Maybe next time." Yet I was not satisfied with simply thinking, "If it doesn't happen, I did the right thing by praying, so I am okay with God." I needed answers. When you use God's Word and faith and pray in the name of Jesus, healing should take place. It is not complicated. So, what was wrong? There had to be answers in the Word.

Suddenly I felt like a woman with a large garden and not a clue where to begin digging for the answers I needed. In fact, I did not even know how to "dig" into the Word. I read Psalms and Proverbs daily and read through the Word at least once a year. That is not uncovering deep truths, though. It's sad to say, but I did not seek the Holy Spirit's help except haphazardly. Yet He is my teacher, and He is there all the time. My answers came over a period of years as truths surfaced, and God helped me piece them together. The answer was not at all what I expected to hear. It was quite a shock.

First, what was Daddy believing for? When someone is not in the Word regularly and seeking the face of God in prayer and allowing changes to happen within, faith is not at a high level. Spending time with God means coming away from that time changed because you become like those with whom you spend time. **If you want to be Christlike, spend some time with Jesus Christ. So, I did.**

From a Wake Up to a Shake Up and More

One day I heard a lady preacher from Australia share a testimony that astounded me. The banana farmers' trees all had blight except for one farmer's. Others did not know why only one farm did not get hit with the plague. He checked it daily. One day he found the beginnings of the disease. Then he sought the Lord diligently, and the disease left. His crop was bountiful. Who changed? He did. Which direction did he go? To God. He did not blame God. He ran to God.

About three years after I had lung surgery to remove the cancerous tumor, a preacher put his hand on my back, and simultaneously I felt a breath escape from within. (I now know it was not a breath; it was the manifestation of a demon leaving my body.) **I could not speak, and the preacher said nothing, but I knew that God had done something, and I knew the preacher knew it, too.** Yet I did not know until that very moment that there had been a reoccurrence of the cancer. I pondered over this awhile, remembering vividly what the Lord had told me when I was watching the movie *The Passion of the Christ.*

When I saw the stripes on Jesus's back, I looked up and said, "Lord, that is why I don't have cancer anymore, isn't it?" Loudly, he said, **"Linda, you will never have cancer again."** I felt like I had been lifted to the ceiling of the theater, I was so thrilled. My spirit was extremely lifted as I bore witness to those precious anointed words. However, twelve months had passed, during which time I'd moved seven times (not because I wanted to but because I yielded to do the will of the Lord)—so how did I end up in this present situation?

Just days later, another preacher told the testimony of the banana farmers, and I received my answer. He said, **"The blight came back, but because you pressed in, I removed it."** The tears would not stop, and I knew without a doubt God spoke those words to me. I had my answer as to why it reoccurred and also **why it was gone! God knows how to get truth surfaced.**

When God said I'd "pressed in," He was not referring to me attending church regularly, or praying regularly, or forgiving regularly. Without anyone telling me, I knew exactly what He was saying. When it is so deep in your spirit that you receive such profound truth, there is no doubt what God is saying. He knows how to get a message through. **He let me know that He knew I'd received the teaching of the Word that took me much deeper than the surface level, the lowest level: the dead letter. I was receiving the living Torah; the Bible came alive like never before.**

No wonder, surface level Bible study, reading, is like putting a sunflower Seed in my mouth, but never cracking the shell to reach the Seed within. That is where the revelation is that brought change in me and I received inner understanding of the Father who gives this gift of revelation. It began changing the way I think, gradually. I was reading Psalm 112:4 the first time this happened to me. "Unto the upright there ariseth light in the darkness: he is gracious, and full of compassion and righteous."

All of a sudden, I thought the grammar was incorrect. I backed up, reread, and *'he'* is referring to the word *'light'*. Sure enough, **I just found Jesus in the Old Testament. No one could wipe the smile off my face.** ☺

God knew I was paying the price to press in. He knew I attended an Apostolic International Ministry, and I was sharing what I was learning with others, yet parting company with them when they chose to compromise. I paid the price not to let my oil get defiled. Mixing oil in a lantern contaminates, and I was guarding my spirit, though it was painful to see so many good friends turn and go back to their old ways. I changed—kept changing, kept digging in the Word, allowed God to set me apart—and my home became not a dungeon or a cell but a throne room where communion with the King of Kings was increasing, as was my love for God.

The more I got to know Him, the more I fell in love with Him. I realized how much carnal knowledge is taught in churches rather than the revealed Word of God as the Holy Spirit brings forth the revelatory Word of God. I learned there are four depths to God's Word and applied what I was taught. The more I listened for hours to accurate teaching on CDs, typing them also, the more content I was to be set apart. I was changing on the inside. My mind-set was changing. **I went from a wake up, to a shakeup, to a turning inside out, to no doubt; the metamorphosis continues, thankfully.**

A metamorphosis was occurring in the realm of the spirit; carnal thinking was replaced with truth revealed by the Holy Spirit as I received it from the apostle who was unveiling the mysteries of God. He fed on what he received directly from God and then taught others what he had received. God's ways are higher. **Breaking through from dead letter to living the Torah brought the illumination of God's glory increasingly.** I was not losing anything except carnal thinking that became replaced with God's way of thinking, His D.N.A., gradually as I submitted to an Apostolic Father and stopped believing lies of many who say 'no more apostles and prophets'. That is not what God says.

Although I was alone, out of the church system, instead of being lonely, I was alone with my best friend. Big difference. **Bottom line:** I did not even know there had been a reoccurrence of the cancer, but God knew, and He loves me so much He healed me as well as let me know why He did so: I'd pressed in. I paid the price to gradually become more perfected as my carnal nature was being replaced with a spiritual impregnation in the womb of my mind with the revelatory Word of God. Did you read that, the womb of my mind? That means men have a womb too, in their mind.

It is so wonderful to learn such truths and dig deeper in the Bible because there is much more. I'm kind of like the new kid on the block so to speak, but I am hooked on teachings that are cracking open the Word of God like this making it new every day and exciting. Apostolic authority is a big key. I needed to learn the importance of submitting to an Apostolic Father as he removed veils and taught me how to do so. The churches sure don't teach it. Not just anyone can teach this level, but *God can connect the obedient to the qualified* to receive that level of spiritual food.

I learned there are at least three more levels in the Word beyond the lowest level which is surface level. I may not be wording all this correctly as God's language births new ways of explaining it; but if I waited until I felt qualified there just isn't enough time. So, I trust the same God that called me, qualified me. I am on fire enough to get this published to help each reader.

If you don't agree with the truth, I don't argue; so just ask the Father to reveal if you are deceived in any way and pray to know truth. Then write a book to help others learn.

If you love God you love people, and do not want anyone going to hell, yet many do, daily. We are accountable to God to use what He teaches us to help others. If we are lazy, that does not excuse the words 2 Timothy 2:15 "Study to shew thyself approved unto God, a workman that needeth not to be ashamed, rightly dividing the word of truth."

When God led me to attend an Apostolic International Ministry I received the teaching I needed. I passed every exam the first time and proceeded to completion in a very brief time period. Fire was in me like never before. I learned not to worry what people think because God called me *out* of the religious system. He had already shown me things that were wrong in the church, and I'd confronted them, but there were no changes. **There was compromise, and that is not God's way.** Jesus did not compromise when He laid down his life for us. We need apostles and prophets and apostolic impartation, and I had tapped in, thankfully.

The more truth I received, the easier it was to stand strong and not compromise. The spiritual battle was intense, but the more free I got, the higher up the mountain I climbed as I stayed hand in hand with Jesus.

I will give one example of my receiving the revelatory Word of God and applying it to my life. You can ask yourself what you would do if this teaching dropped into your spirit and God challenged you to do things His way, rather than the way of the multitudes. **I point out that it is multitudes that will fall away in the end-time—meaning Christians falling away. That is not talking about the world but about carnal Christians falling away, divorcing themselves from God by divorcing themselves from truth. Who? The religious system. That sentence is worth rereading. How do I know? The Bible tells me so.**

Luke 13:27, 28 " But he shall say, I tell you, I know you not whence ye are; depart from me, all ye workers of iniquity. There shall be weeping and gnashing of teeth, when ye shall see Abraham, and Isaac, and Jacob, and all the prophets, in the kingdom of God, and you yourselves thrust out..." The word 'thrust' in Greek 1544 means 'to eject, cast out, pluck, send away'. Pretty serious results. To people calling Jesus Lord, so it is not the world. The church in general is asleep. Carnal teachings and a spirit of slumber go hand in hand. Also, carnal teachings stunt spiritual growth.

When Noah went into the ark it was seven days before the rain came. He had never seen rain. While he was waiting for the rain with his family, listening to a lion roar, a cow moo, a rooster crow, birds chirp, etc. he had opportunity to doubt. I am so thankful he didn't. Perhaps this is where the expression came: "Don't miss the boat." Also, during that seven days no one else got on the ark. (Unless God shut the door when Noah entered, I don't know.) But it is something to think about. We do not have to live in ignorance of truth. To deny truth does not change the truth. My mindset is gradually being transformed by more truth as taught by a very anointed Apostolic Father.

Christmas, I learned, is a pagan holiday. Long story short, my head immediately told me it is to celebrate the birth of Jesus, He is the reason for the season—the words to the Christmas carols came to mind—and so on. So my mind was quick to justify that what I was being told must be wrong...the pagan holiday. **The moment I heard the truth, the battle began, because the mind is the battleground.** *It is a tug of war like never before* because every truth I receive that exposes any wrong thinking is removing deception. Deception is flat out ejected and replaced with God's glory through the truth. Daily I gain back territory that was lost.

I know you thought you were going to read about me being a cancer survivor; well, this is *part of the survival process*, which just happens to be an intense battle in the spiritual realm—a realm that is more real than that which we see with the natural eyes. So please bear with me: I am giving you the answer I received, and I received the truth. God confirmed the truth many times through His Word and in other ways also.

If you want the truth, I am telling you why I don't have cancer. It required something on my part: responsibility, change, accountability, yielding my will, not following the crowd—daring to be different and to be led down a very narrow path. I dared, and I am free—not free from the mouths of religion, but I am free, and John 8:36 **"If the Son therefore shall make you free, ye shall be free indeed."**

So I found myself thinking about the prayer with Daddy and about the time he had been at home yet did not read the Bible or press in. He played literally thousands of games of solitaire to fill time, wearing out many decks of cards—but what would Jesus want him to do? **Our viewpoint needs to mirror God's viewpoint if we are going to be survivors of anything.** Just confessing it does not make it happen. It is like having sex and never getting pregnant. Graphic, I know, but it will get the message through loud and clear. If you have been busy confessing, and it is not happening, it is because you need first to become impregnated with God's Word—grafted in—yet a majority of churches do not respect the fivefold ministry.

When this happens, and the true apostles and prophets are not allowed to do their God-given jobs, the Word of God is not taught according to the interpretation God gives. The more man's natural mind brings forth surface-level teachings, the more off-track church going Christians become. They are deceived because by simply going to church, they think they are doing the right thing—not if milk is fed, which results in the saints remaining baby Christians; God calls everyone to continually be maturing—no complacency, no lukewarmness. Promote the pacifier to the trash can.

If you can see prophetically or symbolically, you will know there will be a falling away before the day of the Lord. Apostasia in Greek means "to fall away or forsake"; it is a deflection from the truth. Falling away is the result of a lack of truth, not the result of people living in the world doing their own thing. The disbelief is because of the lack of truth. At the end of the age, the church is not going to have truth.

The church does not understand scripture anymore. This has created a falling.

Is there something to support that statement? Absolutely, the Bible. 2 Thessalonians 2:11 "And for this cause God shall send them strong delusion, that they should believe a lie: That they all might be damned who believed not the truth, but had pleasure in unrighteousness." Who sends strong delusion? God. God has not changed, He still requires obedience.

Grace does not excuse the necessity to pick up our cross daily, crucify the flesh, and study. Disciples do that. A follower who does not change is not a disciple of Jesus Christ. Thank God, I got woke up, left the religious system, and learned from an Apostolic Father's teachings that are in line with the Early Church Fathers, the truth that set me free. I run forward, not looking back, as I recall one four hour meeting I attended: I learned more than in a year of regular church attendance previously. It was astounding.

I hope you are stirred and have realized what manifests in the natural is what the church is doing in the realm of the spirit. A large percentage of the church has divorced itself from truth, which is a reason there are so many divorces in the world. **People have divorced themselves from truth, resulting in their not having a solid foundation.**

It happened to me, but I pressed in, and God led me to the truth; now my foundation is strong, and I am healthy and staying focused. The fear of the Lord is the beginning of wisdom, and I have much more fear of the Lord after what He taught me concerning cancer and healing and my responsibility to be accountable daily in all areas.

God will give the answers when we press in, but our flesh will not like it one bit. The flesh dies hard. When we have to pay a price, it shows how sincere and how committed we really are...or are not. The Holy Spirit will bring revelation to the church through apostles and prophets. Babies do not have the ability to unveil things; they cannot get that revelation. When the fathers come in and say something is wrong, they show how to clean it up too. Babies do not change babies' diapers. At the end of the age, revelation must occur.

God brought me the teaching I needed to get me on track through an Apostolic International Ministry and that is when I had no qualms about answering God's call to come out of the religious system and shake the dust off my feet against the carnality that was being taught. I did.

The mind-set I have now is far changed because I am getting Jesus unveiled in my life, and I obey Him. I am not learning the commandments of men. I now have understanding, and the beastly nature is being destroyed as I destroy the carnal mentality and replace it with revelatory teaching and apostolic understanding.

The seed is the Word. People are being impregnated by different kinds of seeds. People who are marked in their minds by the carnal nature have *666* on their foreheads because they refuse to deal with it. It is in the head, according to the Greeks; the problem is inside the head, in the way people are thinking. Satan wants everything external because that way you don't have to change.

To change your mind-set, you have to change something. God is talking to everyone, and it is time to get serious with Him and be accountable for our mistakes. Dying to the self is hard yet necessary. When tribulation comes, it proves who you really are. When pressure comes, how do you react to the pressure? Do you love Jesus or betray Jesus? Faith is trust. Do you trust God with your finances and everything else too?

The majority of the church will spend eternity in darkness for lack of understanding if they don't wake up. It is time to wake up and ask God for eyes to see and ears to hear what the Spirit of the Lord is saying. He has called us to worship Him, lay down our lives, and pick up the life of God. We can't do it unless we are taught the truth.

I learned that the truth is that I had the curse of cancer because of my own sin, complacency, lack of understanding, lukewarmness, lack of study in the Word, receipt of false teaching, and all the other reasons I wrote about. **When you are deceived, you do not know it.** To tell self, all is well because the crowd is doing the same as you is to be deceived *because* it is the minority, the remnant, that Jesus is coming for—not the multitudes! The multitudes have fallen away as prophesied in the Word. The Second Coming is very close.

I'm not writing to win friends, so if you don't like the truth, it is not my problem. My responsibility is to please God, and He is pleased when I bring truth. You have been challenged to walk away from carnality and false teaching and answer God's call in your life. The Holy Spirit will lead you, too, if you are teachable, sincere, committed, and accept the truth that the mysteries of God need to be taught, and carnal religious people cannot get the mysteries. **The mysteries are the secret way God governs the righteous, but they are hidden to carnal, wicked, ungodly men.** Are you being taught the mysteries by a true Apostle of the Lord? **Most churches threw the apostolic fathers out.** Pastors in general kept the sheep fed on milk, which results in little growth, yet makes them easy to control. Hello? I lived it, was called out and set free, and now you are being challenged.

Teachings that line up with the Word of God, as well as the Early Church Fathers' teachings are not taught by many true Apostles. God wants your inner man, your spirit, prepared. Will you let Him change you, or are you just waiting, thinking you can be a sinner one second and suddenly be in a glorified body? I don't think so. The multitude was cut off in the day of Noah—so shall it be in the end-time. The carnal nature is demonic, according to James. It is carnal people who do not want to submit. Deuteronomy 28:42 needs to be seen spiritually. **Locusts speak of things that will eat the tree of life; they are spiritual mind-sets.**

This could go on forever, but it is time to finish this chapter and maybe even time for you to read this book again. Why? So seeds of truth are sown into your spirit, and you will know cancer is a sign that you are going in the wrong direction. With all due respect to each reader, I pray you will know the truth and not be deceived. The truth is love; the Word is God's nature, and it is love—not carnal love like we have on this earth.

To not love the truth sets oneself up for a strong delusion followed by condemnation. We can either be molded by the Word of God or put into prison. My prayer is that each of us will be molded into the image of Jesus Christ as we run the race for His glory and for the Word of God to be revealed, sod level.

When for a time, the teaching I needed was not available locally, I reentered the carnal system for several years, went to several churches briefly. I kept my guard up to protect myself from the religious system, while hoping to find deeper truth. Instead I found someone eating a banana and cookies in church during the service, an adult; no correction brought, total disrespect shown. Another church started selling items salvaged from a fire elsewhere so the proprietor could donate the money to the church. Why not give everything away? There was more excitement over the shopping spree after the service than the service itself. Grievous. The Holy Spirit slapped my fingers when I reached to purchase a pair of panty hose for 50 cents at one of the tables displaying items after service. So, help me, if I looked up and saw Jesus with a whip it would not have surprised me. I went to one of the pastors to share my experience and concern for the church in general. My words fell on deaf ears. I moved on.

When you have tasted truth to a deeper level the whole world looks different. Having eyes to see God's way was a whole new dimension. Yet I needed to find an Apostolic Father to teach me, and kept searching only to find religion had flooded many churches with twisted truth by pastors who were in control. Refusing to recognize why the Apostolic Fathers and Prophets were part of God's plan. It was shocking, I knew I had much to learn, but what I saw was not hard to walk out of time and again. Religion is not the answer. Religion is a turn off tool of the enemy, yet recognized by few who call themselves believers of Jesus Christ.

Several years passed. I found that success in business did not fill the void, and "milk" did not cause spiritual growth. Long story short, God called me out and favored me to go to attend teachings led by the preacher that first taught me the deeper levels in the Word of God. I attended meetings out of town for three weeks. Favor, open door, it was like 'Coming Home' after a long season of wilderness wandering and searching. Thinking of Elijah and how protégés choose mentors, not visa versa. Now, thankfully, I am on track, tapped in, submitting to my Apostolic Father and have an understanding of why the church in general is looking for Jesus to return—but that is not what is about to happen as they think.

Remnant means "a few," and the remnants are being prepared because they are not stunted by a surface-level understanding of the Word of God. They have been illuminated and have submitted to an Apostolic Father who is anointed with truth and not afraid to teach it. The church will have the opportunity to wake up, but time is short, and as the Word states that there is a great falling away—that is, by those who knew the Lord. Hello? Heathen don't say, "But Lord, I served you..." It is the church in general crying out like virgins with no oil in their lamps. The lamp is symbolic of the menorah. Hell is real; so is heaven. The decision is made by you. No one else can take you to either heaven or hell. You decide.

I learned that the more I remove carnal thinking and my thoughts and words line up with the Word, the more darkness leaves and is replaced with truth and the glory of God as I become more like Adam before the state of the Fall. No wonder I am excited. Life has purpose, meaning; the Word being taught by an Apostolic Father is causing me to mature as well as learn how to unveil mysteries in the Kingdom of God.

I am not going the route of the grave, either. I am stepping over the grave as I continue to prepare this body with the removal of fleshly, carnal thinking and the receipt of the revelatory word—four levels of the Word. As I learn to dig deep and unveil the mysteries of God, I don't care about TV when the Word has become this exciting. Truth is there to be found if we stay fired up and passionate for the truth—and I am. Hallelujah. I challenge you to seek more truth, too. Illuminated from within, I am—an illuminated overcomer in Christ. Glory to God!

Prayer Points. I speak truth and that is why I will not... tell you to simply pray a sinner's pray. That is all you need to do to become a Christian, and then grace covers you, everything will be all right. That is what the church is saying lately, not true.

I will tell you the church in general teaches that and it is twisted teaching that feeds your carnal nature. The church promotes pampering your flesh, the carnal nature. Jesus teaches that we must carry our cross daily, crucify the flesh, be holy, and His standards do not change. Does your pastor teach any Greek or Hebrew or the importance of learning it? Does he/she refer you to the e-Sword program as a study tool? Does he continually give his opinion rather than bring you Jesus?

Does he talk more about building his house than the body becoming His temple? Does he mock witchcraft, preach more about self than the Word with revelation? Does he teach carnal interpretation of the Word? Does he ask for money to qualify you to receive what he proclaims? Does he keep asking for money but his congregation continues to live in poverty situations and need healing?

Do you recognize manipulation which is a form of witchcraft? Is he condescending with some who rose above his manipulative ways? Does he seek opportunity to humiliate someone publicly? Does he exalt self a lot and name drop? Does he provide updates on projects that received much financial help only when they are thriving? Does he proclaim how difficult it is to forgive?

Does he have a problem with anger, often? Does he have a weak fear of God? Does he talk more about the devil and what he is saying and doing, than Jesus? Does he inform you to give to him personally, financially, means no income tax receipt is issued? Is that fact conveniently omitted, thus you have partial truth, a lie? Does he teach that no one can be perfect? Does he control others easily? Does he talk more about sex than holiness? Do his words exemplify holiness?

Does he tell you we are not under the law, throw out the Old Testament? Does he ever read books by Origin, and other Early Church Fathers whose teachings differ vastly from what is being taught in most churches today? Do you still believe in the rapture? Has the Book of Revelation been unveiled to you by an Apostolic International Ministry as is being done for me? Are you part of the many in church who were lulled to sleep and don't know it, not fearful of the Lord, not changing, not ready, and too deceived to know it?

When you are deceived you don't know it. Are you believing a lie? Are you believing a lie? Worth repeating again, are you believing a lie? How many lies? When you are deceived you do not know it. These truths are piercing through darkness brightly to help you escape the snare of religion and deception. Ask yourself the following questions please. What are you learning?

Do you know the significance of the Shofar; not to mention the Menorah, Outer Court, Holy Place, Holy of Holies? The Feasts of Trumpets, Feast of Atonement, and the Feast of Tabernacle are God's Feasts. Do you celebrate God's Feasts? Are you being taught truth or twisted teachings worse than fake news? Twisted teachings can send you to hell. God requires study of His Word, obedience to His Word. Teaching that lines up with the Early Church Fathers, if teachings of the disciples of Jesus Christ are not accurate enough for you, check your mindset.

I am hitting the nail on the head unashamedly. Why am I so direct? Because I love truth and I care for souls. Do not go into denial, answer those questions honestly and know it is God calling you out of a state of slumber and deception, away from religion and false teachings that feed your carnal nature. The devil wants you to stay snared by religious spirits, so you will be one that hears Jesus say, "I know you not." Wake up Church… It is the Church that fell away, the heathen do not call Jesus 'Lord'.

If you answered yes to most of those questions it is time to **get out of that church fast. God is calling you out, not the devil.** Shake the dust off your feet as a testimony against those who tickle your ears, pamper your flesh, and keep you snared with twisted teachings. Shake the dust off your feet against those who do not fear to use the pulpit to demean someone; let alone teach how to keep the carnal nature satisfied, while killing your spirit with religion. Twisted truth. I know, I was a victim. Was. Is your church parked at Pentecost or are you entering the Promised Land? How much of what you believe lines up with the Bible?

Christians who are obedient to God, celebrate God's feasts. Not the pagan celebrations of Easter and Christmas. Check the origin. To simply celebrate what parents celebrated does not validate the authenticity. Check out teachings by Origin, Early Church Fathers, first 300 years, the standard that was risen. Jesus does not change. He requires much of every believer. Your decisions decide if your eternity is spent in heaven or in hell. Both are very real. *Salvation is a process to be worked out daily.*

To be in covenant with God is a covenant of communication unsurpassable as He reveals through symbolisms, mysteries, secrets, prophecy, His Word, His Son, the Holy Spirit, and the future He has for you. The decision is yours. I leave it up to you to have that prayer from your heart to His. He will meet you where you are at. Just know, serving Jesus Christ will cost you everything, but it will be worth it all. You can never out give Him. I pray His blood shed for you is not in vain. He loves you and I care too. That is why I wrote this book... captives need to be set free. Are you free or do you believe a lie? Leave the comfort zone. Jesus is our example.

Some who call themselves Christians left the church knowing something was wrong, but did not pursue truth. Many are in the church, void of truth. This is a huge wake-up call to the church. My prayer is that you do not experience this: *"Lord, I was a soul winner, etc."* and He says, *"I know you not."*

Ask God to lead you to the true anointed Apostolic Father who will teach you truth. Revelation. Mysteries and secrets, symbolisms, the Word of God. God the Father, Yahweh, responds to a sincere repentant heart. He still forgives in the Name of Jesus/Yahshua. He knows how to get you where you need to be and with whom. Take step one, He will show you step two. Teamwork...Supreme, supernaturally done, ask for Eyes to See spiritually. Fear God, not man. It is decision time.

From Scalpel to Sword: God's Word pierces far deeper than the scalpel, with truth. Scalpel was needed when I had cancer, but limited in effectiveness, sent me home to die in several months. The Sword, Word of God, healed me when an anointed Apostolic Father prayed for me. Scalpel, sword, like from Logos to Rhema, both are needed, but scalpel, like Logos is limited in bringing twelve fruits of the Spirit. (Not nine. That's another wrong teaching.) Are you awake yet? Stirred?

Rhema is needed and only anointed Apostolic Fathers can teach the revelation they receive from God directly. Pastor's cannot. Apostolic Fathers are called to teach the Rhema, deeper revelation, prophetic Word of God, but were denied their position. God is raising up an army to meet this need. What position are you called to? You better find out soon and start running forward. How effective was Elijah? Hell and Heaven are waiting. What is your destination right now? Ask God. Are you ready? Are you sure? Are you believing many lies?

God, Yahoshua, wants you free. God woke you up. Repent, pray, focus, and press in. He led you to read this book. It is not a coincidence. Thank you for reading *Scalpel to Sword*.

Once again, "Wake up Church." My prayer is that you do not experience this: *"Lord, I was a soul winner, etc."* and He says, *"**I know you not**."*

Nugget: Do you know when Jesus is coming? If not; *you are not ready*. Man does not know, but the spirit man does. Mysterious, isn't it? Also, truth.

Shalom,
Linda Lou Jones

www.ingramcontent.com/pod-product-compliance
Lightning Source LLC
Chambersburg PA
CBHW051818090426
42736CB00011B/1544